McCOOK COLLEGE
WITHDRAWN

D1201659

Martin Fierro

THE GAUCHO
MARTIN FIERRO

BY JOSE HERNANDEZ

THE GAUCHO
MARTIN FIERRO

ADAPTED FROM THE SPANISH AND
RENDERED INTO ENGLISH VERSE
BY WALTER OWEN WITH DRAW-
INGS BY ALBERTO GUIRALDES

FARRAR & RINEHART
INCORPORATED
ON MURRAY HILL   NEW YORK

804

6-43

PQ
7797
+3
m32
1936

COPYRIGHT, 1936, BY FARRAR & RINEHART, INC.
PRINTED IN THE UNITED STATES OF AMERICA
ALL RIGHTS RESERVED

THE PREFACE

It is a great satisfaction to me to offer to the great North American reading public, long familiar with tales of the cowboy and the prairie, this poem of the life of the Gaucho Martin Fierro, since the gaucho is but the South American counterpart—as far as such a thing is possible—of the cowboy, and the Pampas on which he lived and had his being are but the South American prairies. Tales of the prairie and the cowboy, his fights with the Red Indian and the hardships of his life, still remain as a tradition of the good old days not much more distant nor less cherished than those of Martin Fierro in South America.

The present edition of my English version of the great national epic of the Argentine is a facsimile reproduction of the text and illustrations of the limited English edition of 450 copies, printed at the Shakespeare Head Press, St. Aldates, and published in August of last year by Basil Blackwell of Oxford. The only alteration in the book is the substitution of the present preface for one that had been written specially for the Oxford publication.

That publication was successful from the outset. His Majesty King Edward VIII, at that time His Royal Highness The Prince of Wales, was graciously pleased to accept the first copy to leave the press, as his personal interest in the River Plate countries, which he has twice visited, is well-known.

Further, shortly after its appearance, this English version was reviewed very favourably by several of the leading newspapers in Great Britain—*The Times* devoting considerable space to it both in the daily edition and in the *Literary Supplement*.

MARTIN FIERRO is no doubt already familiar to many people in the United States through the work of Mr. Henry A. Holmes, Ph.D., Instructor in Romance Languages in New York University, who has shown much understanding of the background and literary value of the poem in his work entitled MARTIN FIERRO: AN EPIC OF THE ARGENTINE (Instituto de las Españas de los Estados Unidos, 1923). I trust, therefore, that this adaptation into English will serve both to illustrate Mr. Holmes' book and will itself benefit from his work as a very full introduction to the life and character of the gaucho.

I, therefore, look forward to my version of the poem receiving a welcome in the United States as warm as that which was accorded to it in Great Britain last year.

THE CONTENTS

PART THE FIRST
THE DEPARTURE OF MARTIN FIERRO

PART THE SECOND
THE RETURN OF MARTIN FIERRO

The Contents

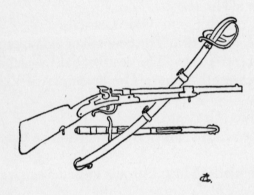

THE INTRODUCTION

BY THE TRANSLATOR

IT is with considerable pleasure that I present this English version of José Hernández's poem, *The Gaucho Martin Fierro*. The first book comprises *La Ida*, or *The Departure* of the hero of the poem, Martin Fierro. The Second Book is entitled *La Vuelta*, or *The Return*.

A translator is not usually expected to preface his labours. The fact, however, that Hernández's poem is unknown to English-speaking people outside of a limited circle in the Argentine and her neighbouring Republics will justify a few words of introduction which otherwise might appear officious.

José Hernández was born on the 10th of November, 1834, on the estancia Pueyrredón, district of San Martin, Province of Buenos Aires, which was the property of the family of his mother, Doña Isabel Pueyrredón, his father being Don Rafael Hernández. His youth and early manhood were passed on the estancia, in the working of which he participated; and it was there that he acquired that intimate knowledge of the environment, social condition, habits, psychology and dialect of the gaucho, which he later employed in defending the gaucho as a class against injustice and in advocating reforms in his social and economic condition.

Like many prominent Argentines of those turbulent times he was by turns, and sometimes simultaneously, estanciero, journalist, politician and soldier. His first journalistic venture was with the *Reforma Politica* in Buenos Aires and later in the town of Paraná. After the defeat of

the 'Confederación' at Pavon, he moved to Corrientes,
where he occupied a number of important public posts
under the Government of Dr Evaristo Lopez. In 1864
he left Corrientes for Rosario; and four years later he
returned to Buenos Aires and founded there the news-
paper, *Rio de la Plata*, in the columns of which he sus-
tained with a facile, fearless and pungent pen his political
and social ideals. When in 1870 the Province of Entre
Rios made a bid for its independence, he closed that paper
and joined the ranks of the Provincial forces. After the
disaster at Naembé he was forced to fly to Montevideo,
and during his stay in that city he co-operated in the
editorship of *La Patria*. At the termination of the Pre-
sidency of Sarmiento, he returned to Buenos Aires, and
was elected Deputy of the Provincial legislature. He died
at the age of fifty-two at his 'quinta' San José, in Belgrano,
one of the suburbs of Buenos Aires.

The First Part of *Martin Fierro* was published by
Hernández in Buenos Aires in December 1872. The
popularity which it attained induced its author to
publish a Second Part, entitled *The Return of Martin
Fierro*, which appeared in 1879, seven years after the
publication of *The Departure*.

During those seven years the First Part had run through
fifteen editions in the Argentine alone, with a total of
some 60,000 copies. *Martin Fierro* had seized upon the
imagination of the gaucho and had stepped out of the
pages of the printed poem to become a living figure, the
embodiment of his hardships and rugged virtues, the
champion of his wrongs, the spokesman of his claim for
social justice. In the rustic 'pulpería,' with its halter-
rutted hitching-rack, its iron-grilled counter and its tra-
ditional 'cuatro frascos,' where the neighbours fore-

gathered at the day's close; in the gaucho's shack with its mud-walls, straw-thatch and raw-hide door-flap; around the lonely camp-fire under the prairie stars; or away on the border outposts where every estancia had its watch-tower and its store of arms, the story of Martin Fierro and his comrade Cruz had been sung and re-sung to the accompaniment of the guitar.

Every gaucho could play the guitar and every gaucho was a singer. And here was no town-bred poet, writing verses full of unfamiliar scenes, literary conceits and long-nebbed words, but one singing as themselves, but better, of the things they knew and saw and felt, in words full-flavoured of the Pampa soil, the rank, gusty, vivid life of plain and ranch and outpost, of round-up and cattle-brand and Indian raid. Fierro and Cruz were flesh and blood. They had gone over to the Indians as the book told, to escape the press-gang and the injustice of a government that daily made a greater fuss over a man's settling his quarrels in the good old-fashioned manner with his 'facón.' Some day they would return, and the gauchos would gather to welcome them. Meanwhile, camp-stores included with their orders for supplies from Buenos Aires, among tins of sardines, crocks of square-face gin, cheese, salt, 'salame,' tobacco, sheath-knives and other staples, 'so many dozen Martin Fierros'; and now and then a gaucho returning from a rare visit to the great city 'where the government lived,' would recount how he had seen with his own eyes Martin Fierro himself, robust and bearded, dressed in town-clothes, and had doffed his hat to him. For José Hernández had become one with his hero, and was familiarly known in the streets of Buenos Aires as 'Don Martin.' But the gaucho audience in the 'pulpería' knew better. Martin Fierro was over the Border.

Some day he would return . . . So Hernández brought him back.

To the reader of *The Return* it will be evident that Hernández in this second part of his poem had determined to make full use of the power which the popularity of his hero had placed in his hands, in order to present a brief for the gaucho class against the corrupt officialdom, which under the aegis of a far-away and negligent Government, and the growing system of absentee-landlordism, was responsible for the injustice and exploitation of which he was the victim. After recounting the sufferings of Martin Fierro and Cruz among the Indians, the customs and mode of life of the tribes,— which form valuable records of the life of the aborigines of the country—and Martin's fight with the Indian brave, which in the original is as realistic as any similar thing in literature, the narrative becomes a series of faithful pictures of the life of the time and place, told by the various characters introduced: the two sons of Fierro, and the son of his old comrade Cruz, who had given his life in an attempt to save a savage benefactor in the great 'never-never' lands beyond the frontier. The unjust judge, the bullying district-officer, the covetous and unscrupulous 'alcalde,' the pitiless commandant, the press-gang, the ration and uniform 'racket' on the frontier, the 'tutors' appointed as cats-paws for thieving officials, the dispersal of families and the sale by faked auction of their goods and chattels, the officer who demands a share of the gambler's spoils as the price of immunity, the farce of judicial process, and the brutality of the staking-yard,— all these are counts in Hernández's arraignment of the system, and were no more than truthful presentations of fact. This didacticism is, inevitably, a literary handicap, but the author has sustained the interest in his poem by colourful atmosphere, vigorous phraseology, witticisms, pieces of folk-lore, homely saws which are often impressed with the peculiar stamp of the gaucho's mentality, and by the full-flavoured tang of dialect.

It is in the untranslatability of the charm of dialect that the present translation suffers the greatest disadvantage. The difficulty is insurmountable; the loss a very real one. To the son of the soil, be he native of Scottish glen, of Devon dale, of Texan prairie, or of the Pampa plain, nothing can replace the homely beauty and the racy vigour of his native speech. Translate dialect into dialect and the incongruities of the implied environment with the characters would make the attempt ridiculous however cunning the translator might be. The dialect localises the characters and they cannot be transplanted without becoming distorted into caricatures.

One portion of the poem which will sound strange to English ears, calls for a few words of explanation. This portion is the 'contra-punto', or singing-match, near the close of the poem, between Martin Fierro and the negro, who turns out to be the brother of one whom Martin Fierro had killed in a 'pulpería' fight years before. The idea of an extemporised singing-contest held in such an environment is apt to appear to us as incongruous, or at the least exotic. But it is no literary device. To-day in Southern Spain, and throughout most of the Republics of South America, in all the lands where the guitar is the instrument of the people, the custom of the 'contra-punto,' or 'payada,' still lingers, though it has passed its heyday. Even to-day in Buenos Aires in places where old-time customs still have their devotees, one may hear at times, when the raucous radio is for a moment stilled, the voice of one of the heirs of the roving troubadours of the past; and the thrum of the guitar forms a murmurous background against which actors in some swift-moving drama of the old gaucho life, with clash of spur, gleam of 'facón' and swirl of poncho, wake to a brief mortality the loves and hopes and hates of times that have gone down the steep. And upon rare occasions, if one is lucky, one may hear a 'payada' in the traditional style, with challenge and acceptance according to rule and canon, and then the song flashing back and forth, criss-cross of question and answer, lunge, parry, and riposte, guitar answering guitar, and the circle of listeners with their 'Bravos!' and their bursts of applause.

In the days before the radio, before the Opera at Buenos Aires was broadcast on the Pampa winds and Lily Pons was on tap in the 'pulpería,' the 'contra-punto' was an institution in the land. Every camp-store had its champion; and travelling singers, coupling often their profession as ranch-hands with their noble art of song, roved here and there, their guitars slung across their shoulders, their ponchos often tattered, but their hearts and lips touched with the fire of poesy, ever ready to make a match with the best, and assured everywhere of a welcome and an audience. Such was the 'payador' Juan Gualberto Godoy, some of whose famous impro- visations were copied out by hand and given away to customers of the 'pulpería' of which he was owner. Juan Manuel de Rosas who became the dictator of the Argen- tine, captured the hearts of the gauchos by his skill as a singer against all comers. And Santos Vega the 'trouvère' par excellence, the captain spirit of them all, has taken his place among the homeric figures of the Pampas. He died of grief after having been defeated in song by a mysterious black-robed stranger under the shade of an 'ombú.' The stranger left a smell of Sulphur, and it was said that he was the devil; and to this day on moonless nights between Dolores and Tuyú a solitary horseman with a guitar across his shoulders passes enveloped in an echo of song—the ghost of Santos Vega.

The subjects of which these old singers sang were not always objective. The gaucho had small book-learning, but he was keen-witted, observant, religious and meditative. Moreover he was the inheritor of the Andalusian tradition, coming down from the middle ages, for whose troubadours matters dealing with religion, morals, philosophy and abstract science were current coin. In song, a cursory treatment, often departing little from a stereotyped form, was all that was possible. The object was to stump the opponent, and it mattered little if his answer was profound or true. What mattered was to show some comprehension of the matter in hand; and wit and grace in giving even a superficial answer or in getting out of the difficulty was enough to avoid defeat. This will be sufficient to explain both the seriousness with which Martin Fierro and his opponent take their match, and the nature of their questions and answers, which without this comment might appear puzzling to the Anglo-Saxon reader of *The Return of Martin Fierro*.

Since the Second Part of *Martin Fierro* was published in 1879, the Poem has run through innumerable editions, both in Spain and in all the Spanish-speaking Republics of America, from the Argentine to Mexico. The cause of its popularity will be sufficiently evident to all who have read the original Spanish, and if I have done my work tolerably well, to readers of the present English version. Hernández wrote out of his own experience, and his poem was recognised at once, both by the Argentine townsman and the gauchos themselves, as a slice out of the vivid and brutal life by which they were surrounded. The gaucho saw, moreover, in Hernández the champion of his wrongs; and in the hero of his poem, Martin Fierro, the prototype of his own hardy race, with all its virtues and vices, its poetry, melancholy, hardihood, courage and prairie-craft. Within a few years after the publication of the poem, its hero Martin Fierro had become a legendary figure of the Argentine Pampas, and many of its pithy maxims and striking metaphors had passed into the current coin of popular speech. As Cunninghame Graham says in *A Vanishing Race:* 'In the long evenings, seated around the fire, passing the *maté* around, the adventures of Martin were sure to be discussed. The gauchos seemed to take him as the embodiment of themselves and all their troubles (surely the greatest proof a poet has of popularity), and talked of him as if at any moment he might lift the mare's hide which acted as door and walk into the hut. Those of the company who could read (not the majority) were wont to read aloud to the unlettered from a well-worn greasy book, printed on flimsy paper in thin and broken type, after extracting the precious books from the recesses of their saddle-bags or from their riding boots. The others got it by heart and then repeated it as a sort of litany.'

Martin Fierro is the embodiment of one of the most peculiar and interesting human types ever evolved by the adaptation of race to environment: the Argentine gaucho. As the Pampa horses were the offspring of the original Arab strain, brought to South America *via* Spain, so the gaucho was the descendant of the hardy soldier-adventurers of Castille and Leon, in whose blood was already some admixture of the Moor, transplanted to the immense plains of the La Plata basin. Under the influence of his new environment, and with a certain intermingling with the aboriginal tribes, the gaucho emerged as a well-defined racial type, a strange mixture of virtues and vices, of culture and savagery. Arrogant and self-respecting, religious, punctilious within the limits of his own peculiar code, he was yet patient under injustice, easily led and impressed by authority, ferocious, callous, brutal, superstitious and improvident. A hard and expert worker at all estancia tasks, he was indolent and unmethodical, and, owing to his disdain of menial labour, disorderly in his habits and half nomadic in his private life. He was sparing in speech as the Redskin of North America, fatalistic as the Oriental, poetic as an Andalusian, phlegmatic as the Teuton, truthful as an Englishman, moody and sensitive as a Slav, hardy as a Viking, childish almost as an African negro, and ferocious and pitiless as the savage Guaycurús of his native plains, who as an old chronicler says, were 'the most turbulent of heathen, who extract their eyelashes to better see the Christians and slay them.' He might well be named the Arab of the Pampas. In no country and at no time, perhaps, has a race existed among which physical courage, intrepidity, indifference to suffering, and endurance have been held in such high esteem. The gaucho's law was his knife, or 'facón,' and the duel was the recognised method of settling either private grievance or disputes over property.

Such was the Argentine gaucho, who in the first generations of Spanish colonization of the lands of the Rio de La Plata pushed out into the vast grazing-lands that stretched from the sweltering jungles of the Chaco

on the North to the arid wind-swept wastes of Patagonia,
and from the Cordillera of the Andes to the Atlantic,
and formed the fighting vanguard of the invading forces
of civilization against the Tobas and Abipones, the
Guaycurús and Payaguas, the Matacos, Guaranies,
Mocobies and other Indian aborigines. It was largely
from the gaucho class that Liniers, Pueyrredón and Al-
zaga collected the forces which repelled the British in-
vasions under Beresford and Whitelocke; and it was the
gaucho, welded and tempered by the iron hand and
scheming brain of Juan Manuel de Rosas, that formed
the sword with which he carved his way to the dictator-
ship of the fledgling Republic—Rosas, who died a refu-
gee in England and lies buried with his daughter in Eng-
lish soil.

The gaucho to-day has almost disappeared. He was a
transitory and local type, destined from the first to be
sacrificed under the wheels of the Juggernaut car of ma-
terial civilization which he dragged into the virgin lands
of the Pampean plain. The railroad has displaced the
bullock-wagon, the motor has crowded out the horse,
the *pulpería* with its *cuatro frascos* has been transformed
into a well-stocked store, often an agency of a Buenos
Aires emporium. The Indians, shorn of war-paint, horse
and lance, hire themselves out as labourers in the sugar
ingenios. The Justice of the Peace with the machinery of
law has banished beyond the pale the summary arbitra-
ment of the *facón*. To kill a man in lawful fight *(en buena
ley)* is no longer a pride, nor even a misfortune *(una
desgracia)*. The *facón* itself, originally a short-sword
with double edge, two spans long, has shrunk to the di-
mensions of a pocket-knife, or at best a dagger. And the
gaucho has shed, to the sorrow of all those who knew

him in his glory, his *botas de potro*, *chiripá*, and clashing *nazarena* spurs, for *bombachas* and *alpargatas* (bag-trousers and jute-soled canvas slippers); and instead of squatting on the ground or on a well-bleached ox-skull, now thrums his guitar and sings the melancholy songs of a time long-dead while seated on an upturned petrol-tin. As Martin Fierro says:

> No wonder I sigh, for the days gone by,
> The times that shall come no more!

It is the clash between the old and the new, between or-ganized society and the individual, the recurring battle of evolution, that forms the background and the under-lying tragedy of Hernández's poem.

However, in Argentina the poem has gained a new glamour, thanks to the writers and other intellectuals who during the last fifteen or twenty years have inaugu-rated a national movement towards intellectual self-determination. They have been quick to grasp and extol the value of this work as a national tradition. An elaborate bibliophile edition was issued by the Association *Amigos del Arte*, which with its rooms in Florida, the Bond Street of Buenos Aires, is one of the many signs of the manner in which artistic and intellectual interests are displacing the pursuit of material progress which un-doubtedly held the leading place in the national life prior to the Great War, culminating with the boom years of 1908-12.

The War, while it shook European culture to its foundation, caused Argentina to look more to herself for intellectual stimulus and inspiration. To-day, though great European writers and artists visit Argentina more frequently than before, and are always welcomed with a judgment perhaps more discriminating than hitherto, there is a continually growing interest of the Argentine people in their own writers, painters, musicians, archi- tects, etc., whose work is beginning to be known over- seas both in Europe and in the United States.

A word now as to the translation itself. I have prefer- red to call it an adaptation instead of a translation, for the reason that it is not, and was not intended to be, verbally faithful to its matrix. Those who know the poem in its original, will realise that a literal translation, although it might provide the translator with a mental exercise, would have little interest except a philological one. It would totally misrepresent to English ears the value of Hernández's poem, and would meet with no acceptance from the general public. The same would be true of an English poem of the same class if literally translated into Spanish.

A large part of *Martin Fierro* is written in gaucho dialect and it contains numerous references to customs, surroundings, pursuits and habits of life, unfamiliar to any except those acquainted with conditions in the Argentine outlands about the close of the last century. To these circumstances, and especially to the difficulty of rendering a passable equivalent of expressions in dialect, is probably due the fact that up to the present no trans- lation in English has been made, nor, as far as I can find out, in any other language.

A translation, especially of verse, in order to have any value as literature, should read like an original work. Clarity and ease are essential, and they are worth pur- chasing at the price of a certain degree of verbal accuracy. To what extent matter can be remodelled, diluted or compressed to fit the selected form, the limit where

liberty becomes licence, is for the translator to deter-
mine; and on the correctness of his judgment depends
his success or failure. A false note, a too unfamiliar image,
a forced simile, the translation of a dead metaphor into a
live one or vice-versa, a reference which plain and im-
mediately comprehensible in the original, is too obscure
in the translation for the reader's intuition to grasp im-
mediately, a halting metre or a forced or feeble rhyme,
any or all of these may be the result of a too faithful ad-
herence to the text. They must be avoided if the authen-
tic voice of the author is to reach the reader through the
medium of another language. But the translation must
remain a translation; that is, it must produce upon the
consciousness of the reader an equivalent *total impression*
to that produced by the original work upon readers in
whose vernacular it was written. I have attempted in the
following pages to sing Martin Fierro's song as he would
have sung it if he had been able to use English with the
same fluency, raciness and vigour as his native idiom.
How far I have succeeded it is for others to judge.

In this translation, then, I have kept consistently to the
purpose of producing a version which reads as if origi-
nally written in English, but which follows as faithfully as
possible the Spanish text. The exigencies of the verse-
form have made it necessary occasionally to insert a
phrase, or to modify slightly a passage here and there.
But I have kept the padding innocuous, and I do not
think I can be charged with having modified to distor-
tion. Certain passages in the original, however, were ob-
scure even to the authorities I consulted, and if I have
interpreted them wrongly I shall welcome correction.
For the rest, the rendering in English of *Martin Fierro*
is a labour which I have carried out chiefly in the hope

that within its province it may help to strengthen under-
standing and good-will between the Argentine people
and the nations which use the English tongue; and
secondly, simply for love of a tale of bygone days, of
things long past and far away, and of a time whose rhythm
seems to keep closer measure with man's heart-beats than
the age that has succeeded it.

I owe a debt of gratitude to a number of persons
in Buenos Aires. Señor Alberto Hernández, a de-
scendant of the poet, allowed me to examine doc-
uments in the possession of his family, and the
Argentine poet and playwright Mr Hector Pedro
Blomberg solved some knotty points presented by obscure
passages. Doctor Diego Ortiz Grognet, Capitan de Fra-
gata Ricardo FitzSimon, Mr John MacCall, Mr Juan de
Marval, Mr Enrique de Marval and Mr T. A. Owen
went to considerable trouble in answering questionnaires
regarding dialect, customs, dress, weapons and other
features of gaucho life of the period of the poem.

I must specially acknowledge my indebtedness to the
fascinating and erudite work by Señor Eleuterio F. Tis-
cornia: *Martin Fierro, comentado y anotado*, published
by the Philological Institute of the Faculty of Philosophy
and Letters of the University of Buenos Aires, which I
found a mine of information.

Last but not least, it is a great pleasure to me to have
my modest work as translator of Hernández's colourful
poem accompanied by the expressive and appropriate
illustrations which have been specially drawn for this
edition by the well-known Argentine artist Señor Al-
berto Guiraldes.

WALTER OWEN.

THE GAUCHO MARTIN FIERRO

Part the First

THE DEPARTURE
OF MARTIN FIERRO

Part the First

THE DEPARTURE OF MARTIN FIERRO

I

I SIT me here to sing my song
To the beat of my old guitar;
For the man whose life is a bitter cup,
With a song may yet his heart lift up,
As the lonely bird on the leafless tree,
That sings 'neath the gloaming star.

May the shining Saints of the heavenly band,
   That sing in the heavenly choir,
      Come down and help me now to tell
      The good and ill that me befell,
And to sing it true to the thrumming strings;
   For such is my desire.

Come down ye Saints that have helpéd me
   In many a perilous pass;
      For my tongue is tied and my eyes grow dim,
      And the man that calls, God answers him,
And brings him home to his own roof-tree,
   Out of many a deep morass.

O many singers have I seen,
   That have won a singer's wreath,
      That have talked a lot as they passed the pot,
      Of the songs they sang and the songs they wrought,
Till their voices rusted in their throats,
   As a knife rusts in its sheath.

Now all that a son of the plains may do,
   To none shall I give best;
      And none may daunt with a windy vaunt,
      Or bristle my scalp with a phantom gaunt,
And as song is free to all that will,—
   I will sing among the rest.

I will sing my song till my breath gives out,
   I will sing when they bury me;
      And singing I'll come where the angels roam
      The rolling plains of their starry home,—
Into this world I came to sing,
   As I sang on my mother's knee.

And let my tongue be glib and sweet,
  My words be not halt nor few,
    And the men to come that I shall not see,
    In days to be will remember me,
By the song I sang in the days gone by,
  That now I sing to you.

In a grassy hollow I'll sit me down,
  And sing of the days long done,
    Like the ancient wind that sighing goes,
    Through the prairie grass, I will sing my woes,
The hands I held and the cards I played,
  And the stakes I lost and won.

'Tis little I have of bookman's craft,
  Yet once let me warm to the swing
    And the lilt and beat of the plainsman's song,—
    I will sing you strong, I will sing you long,
And the words will out like the tumbling rout
  Of waters from a spring.

With my mellow guitar across my knee,
  The flies even give me room,
    And the talk is stilled, and the laugh and jest,
    As I draw the notes from its sounding breast;
The high string sighs, and the middles weep,
  And the low strings mourn and boom.

I am the best of my own at home,
  And better than best afar;
    I have won in song my right of place,
    If any gainsay me;—face to face,
Let him come and better me, song for song,
  Guitar against guitar.

I step not aside from the furrowed track,
   Though they loosen their hilts as they come;
      Let them speak me soft, I will answer soft,
      But the hard may find me a harder oft;
In a fight they have found me as quick as they,
   And quicker far than some.

When trouble's afoot—now Christ me save,
   And Christ me save from sin,—
      I feel my heart grow big and strong,
      And my blood rise up like a rolling song,
For life is a battle, it seems to me,
   That a man must fight to win.

A son am I of the rolling plain,
  oA gaucho born and bred;
      For me the whole great world is small,
      Believe me, my heart can hold it all;
The snake strikes not at my passing foot,
   The sun burns not my head.

I was born on the mighty Pampas' breast,
   As the fish is born in the sea;
      Here was I born and here I live,
      And what seemed good to God to give,
When I came to the world; it will please him too,
   That I take away with me.

And this is my pride: to live as free
   As the bird that cleaves the sky;
      I build no nest on this careworn earth,
      Where sorrow is long, and short is mirth,
And when I am gone none will grieve for me,
   And none care where I lie.

I have kept my feet from trap or trick
  In the risky trails of love;
    I have roamed as free as the winging bird,
    And many a heart my song has stirred,
But my couch is the clover of the plain,
  With the shining stars above.

And every one that hears my song,
  With this he will agree:
    I sought no quarrel, nor drew a knife,
    Save in open fight and to guard my life,
And that all the harm I have done to men
  Was the harm men wished to me.

Then gather around and hearken well
  To a gaucho's doleful story,
    In whose veins the blood of the Pampas runs,
    Who married a wife and begat him sons,
Yet who nevertheless is held by some
  As a bandit grim and gory.

II

O TELL me not of sorrow and pain,
   Of both I have borne my share;
      Let none in saddle be puffed with pride,
      Though with silver stirrups and spurs they ride,
For the smartest horseman oft has gone
   Astride upon Shanks's mare.

And every man, life teaches him
   The things that a man should know.
      The jolts of trouble and knocks of fate
      Will teach him wisdom soon or late,
For nothing can teach a man so much
   As the bitter cup of woe.

With sightless eyes man comes to birth,
   And hope deceives him quick,
      And sorrow grim it follows him,
      Till it catches and rends him limb from limb;
oLa Pucha! how time whacks into one
   Its sore arithmetic.

There was a time when I knew this land
   As the gaucho's own domain;
      With children and wife, he had joy in life,
      And law was kept by the ready knife
Far better than now; alas, no more
   That time shall come again.

I mind me well when the star of dawn
   Gleamed high in the holy sky,
      And the cock's shrill crow and the cattle's low
      Rose up like a hail in the morning glow,
How the hands to the kitchen's cheery blaze,
   In the paling dusk went by.

They would gather there the blaze around,
　　Till the sun rose round and red;
　　　The kettle sang, and piping hot,
　　　∘They sucked at the circling 'maté' pot,
　∘While their 'chinas,' rolled in their 'poncho's' folds,
　　Lay snugly yet abed.

And scarcely daybreak's red had paled
　　To the blue of the full-blown dawn,
　　　And the birds to sing as they took to wing,
　　　And the hens began their foraging,
　When each with a cheery hail went off,
　　And the morning's work was on.

And one ties on his jingling spurs,
　　And is off with a merry hail,
　　　One looks about for a supple hide,
　　　Or a whip or a lasso, while outside,
　The whinnying colts to their riders call,
　　And stamp at the hitching-rail.

The breaker-in with a lissom stride,
  Unbarred the stockyard gate,
    And while he was fresh, picked the wildest flesh,
    And threw him deft with the lasso's mesh,
And the colt would thrash in the swirling dust
  Like a thing of living hate.

And there the gaucho edged him in,
  And pinned the plunging head;
    They saddled him quick and gave him a lick,
    And the breaker swung to the saddle slick,—
Ah, those were the times when the gaucho showed
  The craft that is in him bred.

And through the gap of the open gate
  Went thundering horse and man,
    A batter of hoofs and a cloud of dust,
    A flurry of fight and rage and lust,
And thrashing leather and raking spurs,—
  Till he stretched his neck and ran.

McCook Community College

Ah times agone! To see them ride
   Was a goodly sight and grand;
      There was wilder horse-flesh then than now,
      And the men were hardier too, I trow,
For never a breaker but got him down,
   With the halter in his hand.

oAnd while some bridled the 'pampa' colts,
   And drilled them to knee and rein,
      The rangers went off in twos and threes,
      Their ponchos aflap in the morning breeze,
To part the cattle and round the herds
   Afar on the grassy plain.

And when the spark of the gloaming star
  Was lit in the paling blue,
    At the kitchen door they came dropping in,
    And many a stirring tale they'd spin,
  As with song and laugh and jest and chaff
  Round the blazing logs they drew.

Till with crops well-gorged with meat and wine,
  When the embered fire grew dim,
    Each doffed his jacket and boots and belt,
    And snugged him down on a fleecy pelt,
  With his 'china' beside him; many a lord
  Might well have envied him.

Ah, my mind goes back and I see again
  The gaucho I knew of old;
    He picked his mount, and was ready aye,
    To sing or fight, and for work or play,
  And even the poorest one was rich
  In the things not bought with gold.

The neediest gaucho in the land,
  That had least of goods and gear,
    Could show a troop of a single strain,
    And rode with a silver-studded rein,
  The plains were brown with the grazing herds,
  And everywhere was cheer.

And when the time of the branding came,
  It did one good to see
    How the hand was quick and the eye was true,
    When the steers they threw with the long lassoo,
  And the merry band that the years have swept
  Like leaves from the autumn tree.

There was work for all—or rather play,
  For a goodly game was yon;
    The plain below, and the sky above,
    A horse and a thatch and a bit o' love,
And a nap in the shade in the heat of day,
  And a dram from the demijohn.

For the demijohn of the wagon-boss
  Swang under the wagon seat,
    And the gaucho spry was not slow or shy
    To tip it up when he felt him dry
They would swig away at its juicy neck
  As an orphan swigs the teat.

What times we had, and what games we played!
  In the days of the cattle-brand;
    We made new friends for the friends we missed,
    And quarrels were settled and wenches kissed,
For the countryside came riding in
  To lend a helping hand.

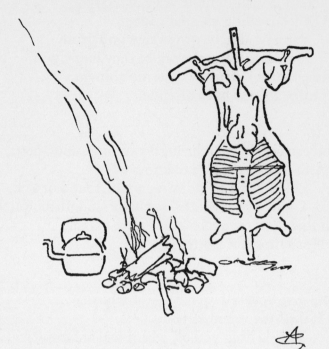

The women folk had lots to do
  From early dawn till night,
    To get the food for the hungry brood,
    They hustled and chattered and baked and stewed,
For there's nought like a day in the branding yard
  To whet the appetite.

There was porridge of corn in steaming pots,
  And fresh-baked bread galore,
    ○And broth and stew, and a barbecue,
    ○And caña or wine as it suited you,
No wonder I sigh for the days gone by,
  The times that shall come no more,

When by favour of none the gaucho rode
　O'er the rolling pampas wide;
　　But now alas, he grows sour and grim,
　　For the law and the police they harry him,
And either the Army would rope him in,
　Or the Sheriff have his hide.

You can hardly step through your own door-posts,
　And the Mayor gets to know—
　　Like a hawk he's down on you, sound or sick,
　　Though your wife has her baby a month too quick,—
Ah there's never a thong but gives at last,
　Nor a time but has to go!

And give yourself up for lost, my boys,
　If the Mayor nooses you;
　　They'll drag you off with a hail of blows,
　　Though why neither God nor the Mayor
　　　knows,
And they finish you quick if you stand and draw,
　As the gaucho used to do.

And blue and black they drub your back,
　And over the head they rap you,
　　And then all sore and smothered in gore,
　　They truss you up and they give you more,
And elbow to elbow tethered tight,
　oIn the filthy stocks they clap you.

And there God knows, your share of woes
  With a vengeance you begin;
    In a cell you'll stay for many a day,
    Till your turn comes round, and yea, or nay,
They draft you off to a frontier post,—
  Thank God you've saved your skin!

It was there, I own, that I learned to groan,
  And thus my griefs began,
    In other songs, if you'll bear with me,
    I'll tell you the tale of my misery;
From the law's grim trap not the Saints of heaven
  Have ever saved a man.

III

'TWAS long ago that with wife and sons,
　　And cattle a goodly batch,
　　　I rode my horse among the best;
　　　But into the army I was pressed,
And when I came back, of all I owned,
　　There was only walls and thatch.

Ah, happy was I 'neath my 'rancho's' roof,
　　As the bird in its feathered nest;
　　　My heart rose up with a father's pride,
　　　As I watched my boys with the rangers ride,
Alas, of all by an evil chance,
　　In a day I was dispossessed.

When work was o'er, in the village store,
　　'Twas my delight to sing.
　　　I would warm my throat with a glass or two,
　　　And sing as now I sing to you,
When I'm primed, the couplets bubble out
　　Like water from a spring.

And once at a merry gathering,
　　I was warm and going strong,
　　　When all of a sudden there and then,
　　　The Justice came with a troop of men,
And the party came to a sudden end;
　　For they took the lot along.

Though some that had been in the trap before,
　　Made off and got clear away,
　　　Like a simpleton I waited there;
　　　I knew I had no accounts to square,
And I wouldn't run; but I soon found out
　　That I was a fool to stay.

oA gringo hurdy-gurdy man,
  With a dancing monkey there,
    Was doing his bit to help the fun;
    They roped him too, though he tried to run;
  A big soft-looking fellow was he,—
  And he cried for sheer despair.

oAnd an English digger of ditches too,
  That had dodged the draft before,
    By telling the Justice, I understand,
    oThat he came from 'Inca-la-Perra' land,—
  He took to his heels and got to the hills
  By the skin of his teeth, no more.

Not even the lookers-on were spared
   In the drive they made that day,
      They made no bones about right or wrong,
      But all they laid hands on they hustled along,
Save one that to please the barkeep's wife,
   The sergeant let get away.

They formed us up at the door and said
   We must serve the Government;
      And they mixed us up with a wretched lot
      That at some other place they'd caught;
Not the devil himself, it seems to me,
   Could anything worse invent.

I knew the Judge had a down on me,
   For I'm no politician;
      On voting day I had stayed away,
      And somebody since had heard him say
That those that didn't vote for him
   Were helping the opposition.

And so no doubt I was ruined there
   At a game where I held no hand,
      For whether the lists be bad or good,
      At the polls there's always trouble brewed,
And I stay away, for I've got no use
   For things I don't understand.

And before we went off, the Judge he up
   And made us a long harangue;
      He said they'd treat us like gallant men,
      And he promised us over and over again,
That we'd only serve six months and then,
   He'd send the relieving gang.

∘I took a 'moro' horse I had,
　A horse in a hundred score,—
　　∘At Ayacucho I made him run,
　　And a pot of money for me he won;
A gaucho with a horse like that,
　Gets credit at any store.

I loaded up without more ado
　∘All that I had in my shack:
　　Saddle-cloths, poncho, all I'd got,
　　I bundled up and lifted the lot;
I scarcely left my wife that day,
　The clothes upon her back.

I'd a full rig-out of riding gear,
   And I took it all along:
      Saddle, head-stall and reins, all new;
     ○Bolas lasso and halter too.
When to-day you see me so poor, may be
   You won't believe my song.

And so astride my 'moro' soon,
   To the frontier I was gone.
     ·To keep a dog would have been a sin
     In the filthy hovels they shoved us in;
I wouldn't have envied one of the rats
   That lived in holes like yon.

Of the wretched crew already there
   Not one did they reprieve;
     The oldest one of the lot complained,
     But a staking-out was all he gained,
And never another word was heard,—
   As you may well believe.

At roll-call that same afternoon,
   The Chief made a speech and said
     That there we were, and there we'd stay,
     And if anyone tried to break away,
The least he'd get was five hundred straight,
   And could give himself up for dead.

Not a single weapon he handed out,
   But for that he was not to blame;
     The Colonel kept all the arms, you see,
     Shut up in his room under lock and key,
To serve to the Army—which was we—
   The day that the Indians came.

They let us alone the first few days,
   To idle and lie around;
   But after that, I can scarcely tell
     oWhat happened. Barajo! that was hell!
They started to treat us, every one,
   Much worse than a mangy hound.

It was whack with the flat if you moved too slow,
   And whack if you moved too quick;
     And if you stood still they called the guard,
     oAnd it was you for the staking-yard;
And the staking or stocking they gave you there,
   For a week it left you sick.

And talk about serving the Government,
   And putting down Indian ravages!—
     We never set eyes on barracks nor arms,
     But the Colonel sent us to work on his farms,
And we left the cattle to wander about,
   And be driven off by the savages.

To make a beginning I sowed some wheat;
   oThen they set me to make a 'corral';
     oI cut adobe to build a shack,—
     La Pucha! they nearly broke my back.
I made a stockade,—but of any pay
   oI touched not a damned 'real.'

And the worst of it was that if you kicked,
   They soon had you down and trussed;
     I tell you they kept us on the run,
     If ever was hell, then that was one;
If they call that serving the Government,
   Then Government can go bust!

A year or more they kept us there
　　At work on the Chief's plantations,
　　　　And I'd be surprised if the Indians knew
　　　　We were there at all; for in they blew
Whenever they liked; and they rounded the herds
　　Within sight of the frontier stations.

At times the patrol-troop came in,
　　They would give tne post a scare.
　　　　The Indians were over, they said, for cert;
　　　　And the guard had better be well alert,—
.They had seen the trail of a cattle-drive,
　　Or the corpse of a putrid mare.

Then they'd send the order round the farms:
　　To arms! To repel the raid!
　　　　And we'd straggle in on our saddle-less nags,
　　　　Some two a-back, and most in rags,
And never a weapon among the lot—
　　The bold Frontier Brigade!

And when we were in; for the sake of show,
　　With a terrible bustle and fuss,
　　　　They beat tattoo, and a trumpet blew,
　　　　And some army drill they put us through;
But what the instructor had never learnt,
　　He could hardly teach to us.

And they lined us up and gave out the arms,
　　And told every one his position,—
　　　　A bundle of lances, some short, some long,
　　　　With rusty points tied on with thong,
And a few blunt swords,—they didn't give guns,
　　Because there was no ammunition.

Though once when I happened to have a chat
  With the sergeant when he was tight,
    He told me the Government sent them ball,
    And powder too, but they kept it all
To sell to the ostrich-hunters there,
  That banged away day and night.

And when the raid was past and done,
  And the Indians got clear away,
    In a terrible hurry we'd bundle out,
    Ill-horsed and half-armed,—a ragged rout,
To follow them up . . . what they'd left behind,
  They came for some other day.

It's there one knows of tears and woes,
  And enough of pains and ills;
    The jaguar's law is the Indian way,
    He shows no mercy:—Be slain, or slay!
He carries off all he can load or drive,—
  What he leaves, he burns or kills.

Not even the babes in their mothers' arms
  Can soften his pitiless bowels;
    Young and old are the same to him,
    He will tear an infant limb from limb,—
The Indian settles everything
  With his spear and a burst of howls.

Your flesh would shake if you could see
  The Indian horde come flying,
    With hair astream in their furious flight,
    ○Loose rein in left and lance in right,
Like a howling blast they are gone, and leave
  A trail of the dead and dying.

From the outer wilds on his wiry horse
    He takes the trackless way;
        He eats the prairie, league on league,
        He recks not hunger or fatigue;
    The Indian and the ant—these two
    Are busy night and day.

At handling the 'bolas' there's nobody else
    As the Indian so clever;
        When you're drawing off,& you think he's through,
        He'll send a chance shot after you,
    And if it catches you, for sure,
    It lays you out forever.

And tough as a turtle the Indian is
    To kill with thrust or slash.
        Though you loose his tripes with a belly-rip,
        He'll shift his lance to his bridle-grip,
    And stuff them back with his hand, and wheel,
    And be off like a lightning flash.

They came as they liked and went as they liked,
    As a hawk swoops on its prey;
        They carried the women off, poor things,
        God knows we cried for their sufferings;
    It was said they used to flay their feet,
    To keep them from running away.

Full sore were our hearts, you may well believe,
    As we followed that track of woe;
        Their mounts went fleet as the Pampa wind,
        While we shambled slowly far behind,
    On a lot of crocked and spavined nags
    That scarce at a trot could go.

And so at the end of a day or two,
Our nondescript brigade
To our frontier station would hobble back,
With our horses dropping along the track,
And we'd drive in the beasts, for the Chief to sell,
That had somehow escaped the raid.

But our luck, I guess, couldn't always hold—
Now good, now ill Fate serves,—
And once the Indians turned on us,
And they lanced us up so barbarous,
That most of us from then began
To suffer from jumpy nerves.

They waited for us behind a hill,
And there the mess began.
Your comrade Fierro felt none too good,
When he heard the howls of that devil's brood;
∘At the bang of a gong they came popping out
∘Like maize in the toasting-pan.

We made ready for them as they came on,
And a fearsome lot they were;
We rallied together our straggling men,
And we rode at them—we were one to ten—
They whooped and howled and shook their spears,
And the wind streamed through their hair.

They shook the ground like a herd of steer,
And I'll say here with no frills,
That though I'm not backward in a fight,
That time I was pretty near a fright,—
I was riding a half-tamed runaway
That I had balled in the hills.

They came with a din of yells and howls
That fairly bristled our hairs;
Like the wind they came, and there we met,
I think I can see those devils yet—
And we broke before them over the plain,
Like a troop of startled mares.

What mounts the sons of Satan had!
Not even to fly we'd a chance.
Like streaks of light their horses were;
They dashed among us here and there;
Each picked the ones that he liked the best,
And spitted them with his lance.

If the Indian gets you with the lance,
You can lay long odds you squawk;
And even a prick will make you sick,
There's nothing known will heal it quick.
We could face them as well as the pigeon can,
The swoop of the sparrow-hawk.

To see an Indian handle the lance
Is a thing to admire, I'll say;
They never let up when they're after you,—
I broke from the mill with some other few,
We nearly went over our horses' ears
In our hurry to get away.

And to cap my troubles, an Indian came
Spitting out foam like a puma;
He rushed at me like a howling gust,
With his lance all ready to give the thrust,
And he yelled out 'Christian, die! Metau
oEl lanza hasta el pluma!'

Lying along on his horse's ribs,
　　Shaking above his head
　　　○A lance like a lasso, he rushed at me;
　　　It was me or him, it was plain to see;
If I hadn't been ready, I tell you boys,
　　He had me as good as dead.

If I had faltered or lost my head,
　　I wouldn't have got away.
　　　I never had much use for fear,
　　　But I don't mind telling you now and here,
My heart began to bubble and shake
　○Like the throat of a toad that day.

The lust he had to have my blood,
　　May God forgive his soul;
　　　I cheated the lance with plunge and rear,
　　　○While I loosed the 'Three Marias' here,
If I hadn't brought 'bolas,' La Pucha! I'm sure
　　I'd never have got home whole.

He nearly had me once or twice,
　　As we circled round and round;
　　　○They told me he was a cacique's son—
　　　Anyway there we pranced and spun,
Until at last with a lucky cast,
　　I tumbled him on the ground.

He was scarcely down when off my horse
　　I leapt, and firm and fast
　　　I planted my foot on his shoulder-bone,
　　　○And although he squirmed, my keen 'facón'
Soon made an end of the saintly work
　　Of making him kick his last.

oI left him there like a boundary-mark,
I swung myself on his horse;
They gave me chase and pressed me near,
But my mount was a winner and won me clear;
God helped me out of that perilous pass,—
May he never send me worse.

McCook Community College

IV

AND now I'll take up my tale again,
    And I hope I don't weary you;
        I need hardly say that since that day
    I began to think of a get-away;
And glad I was to have saved my hide
    From the scrapes that I'd been through.

I'll nothing say about our pay,
    For never a cent we smelt;
        It kept far ahead like the Indian raid,
        Nor even stayed for an ambuscade;
Like a hungry pack we hung on its track,
    But we never got its pelt.

And the filthy state we soon were in,
    Was horrible to see;
        For pity's sake one's heart might break,
        By Christ! it might give you a belly-ache,
I never in all my bitch of a life
    Saw greater misery.

I hadn't even a shirt to my back,
    Nor a rag that looked like one.
        The tatters that were my whole attire
        Would hardly make tinder to light a fire;
You never knew a wretcheder crew
    Than a frontier garrison.

Bridle, buttons, and ornaments,
    Poncho and saddle-mats,
        Little by little I left in the store,
        And once they went in they came out no more,
And I myself was half silly soon,
    With hunger, dirt, and rats.

I had only a ragged blanket left,
  ○That at 'taba' I won one day;
      Of everything else I had been fleeced;
      It kept me from showing my rump at least;
But the ticks in it!—not with a ticket of leave
    Would one of them go away.

And as if I hadn't bad luck enough,
    I lost my 'moro' too;
      The Chief looked him over from tail to head,
      'You don't need a horse like that,' he said;
○'I'll teach him eat grain.' So that was that,
    And what could a poor man do?

Just fancy then my pitiful plight—
    On foot without a horse;
      My navel shewed, my back was bare,
      A filthy rag was all my wear;
If by chance they had wanted to punish me,
    They couldn't have served me worse.

For many a month my wretched lot
    With fortitude I bore,
      Till the year went out and a new year came,
      While everything went on just the same,
Though it seemed to get worse as time went on,
    Like rubbing an open sore.

The only relief we gauchos got,
    That served in the frontier forces,
      Was when of a morning they let us out,
      As long as no Indians were about;
At throwing the 'bolas' we'd pass the time,
    And laming the government horses.

And we'd straggle back along the track
  With our horses winded sore.
    Some ostrich feathers we might bring in,
    Or if we were lucky, perhaps a skin,
That we'd trade for what we needed most,
  With the rascal that ran the store.

The Colonel's bosom friend was he,
  And a thundering barefaced thief.
    He sold his goods at a sinful rate,—
    When we brought him feathers 'twas weight for weight
Of tobacco or 'yerba';—everyone knew
  That he halved what he made with the Chief.

○Four grimy flasks and some empty casks
  Was all that one ever saw there;
    But all you could pay for in goods or cash,
    He'd get you quick, though most was trash;
It almost made one think sometimes
  That he was the army purveyor.

Not a thing was he short of—the swindling rogue!
  And the way he drank was a sin.
    The 'Bar of Justice' we called his place;
    ○Aijuna! I loathed his foxy face,
A cunninger rascal never yet
  Got rich out of watered gin.

It's right that a seller should get his cost,
  And something more besides,
    But he plundered us worse than an Indian raid,
    For with only four bottles as stock-in-trade,
Wagon on wagon he loaded up
  With feathers, furs, and hides.

He kept an account for each of us
  ○As long as a rosary;
    And when a rumour got about
    That our pay had arrived, he got them out;
But some fox must have swallowed the money-bag,
  For not a cent did we see.

But after many a false alarm,
  When the rumours were old and stale,
    They called us all to the store one day,
    And a bounty there they began to pay;
It wasn't until they saw the cash,
  That any believed the tale.

Some took out the clothes they had in pawn,
  Some drank to the Government,
    And others found that what they drew
    Just paid their bills that were overdue;
In the end the bandit that sold the drinks
  Remained with every cent.

I didn't want to hurry them,
  So I put on a waiting air.
    I loitered in and out of the shop,
    And I leant up against a wooden prop.
Waiting for them to call my name,
  To go up and get my share.

And there against that wooden beam
  I might have been leaning yet.
    When the hour of vespers came along,
    I began to suspect there was something wrong;
I thought perhaps they'd forgotten me,
  And I came out all in a sweat.

To get my trouble off my chest,
  And find out what was what,
    I sidled up to the Major there,
    And I said to him with a careless air:
'I suppose to-morrow they'll come again,
  And finish paying the lot.'

'Neither to-morrow nor any day else,
  You greedy animal;
    The pay is finished, and that's the lot,'
    The Major answered me on the spot.
I laughed and I said: 'There's some mistake,
  For I haven't received a 'real.'

The Major looked me up and down,
　And his eyes grew as big as your fist;
　　　I thought they were going to pop right out,
　　　And he shouted at me: 'You stupid lout!
What pay do you think you are going to get,
　If your name isn't in the list?'

I thought to myself 'Well, that's the end,
　When a soldier has no rights;
　　　For a full two years at the post I've been,
　　　And never a pay-day have I seen;
I don't get into the wages list,
　But I get into all the fights.'

I saw that things were looking black,
　So I thought it best to go;
　　　It's unlucky to start an argument
　　　With men that are in the Government;
That's one of the lessons I have learnt
　In the bitter school of woe.

The Commandant somehow heard the tale,
　And he called me up to declare.
　　　He said he wanted to find out well
　　　If anyone hadn't had justice,—Hell!
∘We weren't living in Rosas' time,
　And things were on the square.

The sergeant and the corporal
　Were to head the investigation;
　　　And they started out to verify
　　　Who brought me there, and when, and why,
And the colour and brand of the horse I rode
　The day I arrived at the station.

And soon they were splashing ink about,
　And a terrible fuss were making;
　　It was plain to me they were only bluffing,
　　And making a pie with my pay for stuffing;
But if I'd appealed to the Colonel,
　He'd have made me roar with a staking.

The sons of bitches! I hope their greed
　May finish by bursting their bags;
　　They grudge a poor soldier his tobacco,
　　∘They keep him as lean as a starving guanaco,
And they even swindle him out of his pay,
　And keep him in filth and rags.

But what could I do against them all?
　They were up to every trick.
　　They'd have heeded me as much, or less,
　　Than an ostrich chick in the wilderness;
If I hadn't let on I was half asleep,
　They'd have settled me good and quick.

V

I SAW I might starve for all they cared,
  I began to get desperate then;
    And for many and many a day I prayed
    The Indians would give us another raid,
And in the rumpus I'd get away,
  And make for my home again.

For all we did, the Government
  Might have left the frontier alone;
    In our filthy hutches we lived like rats,
    And the bosses hunted us round like cats;
You might play 'taba' just as well,
  With a loaded knuckle-bone.

Everything yonder is upside down,
　oSoldiers are turned into 'peones';
　　　When the Indians come they call them to arms,
　　　But meanwhile they send them to work on the farms,
And their army pay and their hire as well,
　Is bagged by the Chief and his cronies.

Soldiers and cattle and lands and cash,
　All join in the frontier dance;
　　　There's many a Chief with herds and lands,
　　　And soldiers instead of hired hands,
And many a dirty deal I've seen,
　In spite of my ignorance.

It seems to me they keep up the war
　As a blind to make off with the booty;
　　　If a Chief makes the Army his career,
　　　He's got no call to own the frontier;
He's all rigged out if he's got his horse,
　His poncho, his sword and his duty.

That they didn't intend to let us go,
　As time wore on was plain;
　　　I saw I might stick there till I died,
　　　And I'd never get off unless I tried,
So I fixed with myself I'd watch my chance,
　And make for my home again.

And to put the cap on it, one night,
　What a staking-out they fetched me!
　　　They nearly pulled me to bits, by Gad!
　　　Because of a bit of a row I had;
Aijuna! there in the staking-yard,
　Like a fresh-peeled hide they stretched me.

In my life I'll bet I'll not forget
  What happened to me that night
    At the gate of the fort a raw recruit
    Nearly did for me—the drunken brute!—
Though he propped himself up with his musket, yet
  He could hardly stand upright.

He spoke so thick that no-one there
  Could understand his lingo;
    God knows where they could have found the man;
    I doubt he was even a Christian;
∘A 'papolitano' he said he was,—
  Which I take is a kind of gringo.

They had put him there as a sentinel,—
  The drunken gringo beast,—
    He was soused so well he could scarcely see,
    And when I came up he challenged me;
And the rumpus began when the fool took fright;
  ∘And I was the duck of the feast.

∘He yelled at me: 'Quen vívore?'
  ∘And I answered: 'Qué víboras!'
    I could see him peering about in the dark;
    ∘'Ha garto!' he roared; and just for a lark,
∘I said, 'The only "lagarto" here,
  Is yourself, you gringo ass.'

And on the spot—Christ save my soul!
  I nearly went to glory;
    I heard a click and I ducked my head,
    And he missed me with half a pound of lead;
If he hadn't been too drunk to aim,
  I shouldn't be telling the story.

You may bet the bee-hive was soon a-hum
　At the shot that nearly bagged me;
　　The officers came tumbling out
　　To see what the row was all about;
They left the gringo at his post,
　And off to the stakes they dragged me.

Between a squad with bayonets fixed,
　On the ground they made me lay;
　　The Major half-squiffed came up to see,
　　And there he started to roar at me:
'Aha, you rogue! I'll teach you now,
　To go about claiming your pay!'

Then to my hands and feet they tied
　Four thongs of plaited hide.
　　They hauled and jerked till they gave me hell,
　　But they didn't jerk out a single yell;
And all night long that gringo brute
　With curse on curse I plied.

I'd like to know why the Government
    Enlist that gringo crew,
        And what they think they're good for here?
        They can't mount a horse or rope a steer,
And somebody's got to help them out
    In everything they do.

I can only think they're sent to us
    As punishment for our sins.
        They can't put on a saddle straight;
        To kill a sheep they're too delicate,
And I've seen them shy of a trussed-up calf,
    For fear it might kick their shins.

And they spend their time sitting beak to beak
    And jabbering fool affairs.
        They're always first when it's time to eat,
        But they've got to be shown how to cut their meat
La Pucha! you'd think they were rich men's sons,
    The way they put on airs.

If the weather's hot they're good for nought,
    If it's cold they begin to shiver;
        They'll never buy themselves a smoke,
        But they'll empty anyone else's poke,
And they'll wrangle over a hank of twist
    Without any shame whatever.

When it rains the gringo huddles up
    Like a thunder-frightened hound;
        When there's work to be done they'll stay behind,
        And wag their tongues with the womenkind,
And they'll lift your poncho as soon as wink,
    If you leave it lying around.

At keeping watch they're a wall-eyed bunch,
   You can't teach them anyhow.
      If they're bad by day, they're worse by night,
      You'd think the fools had lost their sight;
They can't tell a horseman from a steer,
   Or an ostrich from a cow.

And when there's a raid it's all clatter and fuss,
   And holding a talking-match;
      And when at last they do set out,
      They're soon dead beat and straggling about;
It's no more use to send them here,
   Than to give a cat eggs to hatch.

VI

AND now begins the saddest part
  Of my tale of trouble and grief,
  Although the whole of my life, God knows,
  Has been nothing more than a chain of woes
Yet the suffering soul that sings its dole,
  In singing finds relief.

Like this it fell: at the time I tell,
  They began to round up the horses;
  They called in all the soldiers too,
  And began to drill them with great to-do,
For a general sally along the line,
  Of all the frontier forces.

They told us we were to travel light,
　　And do leagues and leagues a day;
　　　　We'd fall on the Indians by surprise,
　　　　Before they'd ever a chance to rise,
And when we got back, they'd sign us off,—
　　And that was to be our pay.

And the Chief he made a speech and said
　　We ought to be confident
　　　　That we'd finish the Indians once for all,
　　　　For we were to have, as our General,
○Don Gainza—a Minister, I think,
　　Who was high in the Government.

They said he was calling the army out,
　　Down to the last recruit;
　　　　And they said with cannons we'd be supplied,
　　　　○With a lot of new-fangled scores inside;
La Pucha! if talk could have won the war,
　　They wouldn't have had to shoot.

But they couldn't catch me in a trap like that.
　　I thought it a fool idea;
　　　　And what does a roaming gaucho care
　　　　If a Minister travels here or there?
And as for scores,—I had lots myself,
　○In the books of the 'pulpería.'

I was never a loafer or a fool,
　　But a gaucho ready-handed.
　　　　'Qué Cristo'! of all the things I've dared,
　　　　Not a single one has had me scared;
Though I've often gone over Fortune's ears,
　○On my feet I've always landed.

Since the day I could climb on a horse's back,
  For myself I've had to fend,
    Though little I've had but knocks from Fate,
    And often my plight has been desperate;
Yet of want and woe, 'Barajo!' you know,
  One gets fed up in the end.

Though little I know, I know enough
  To know I'm a good-for-nought;
    I play the hare or I play the hound,
    As Fortune turns her merry-go-round;
But I think it's time that the Government
  Should pity the gaucho's lot.

One night when the Justice and the Chief
  Were close in confabulation, —
    Passing a bottle to and fro,
    I thought I'd risk a chance, and so—
On a horse I caught, like a trail of smoke,
  I faded out from the station.

The desert for me is a bed of flowers,
  When I have my liberty,
    With a knife, a lasso, and a horse,
    Wherever I will I set my course,
And the trackless plain on the darkest night,
  Is an open trail for me.

I've carried my life at my belt so long,
  That I laugh at peril and pain.
    I don't turn tail at the first assault,
    And to find my way I'm never at fault;
○And soon I saw by the lie of the land,
  I was nearing my home again.

'Twas three long years since I'd left my home,
  Three years of woe and care;
    I was scarred with sorrow, want, and pain,
    But ready to try my luck again,
○And as the 'peludo' makes for its hole,
  I headed for my lair.

Only a few bare poles were left,
  And the thatch and nothing more;
    Christ knows it was a mournful sight,
    It withered my heart up like a blight,
And there in the wreck of my ruined home,
  To be revenged I swore.

There isn't a man wouldn't do the same,
  If he'd suffered as much as me;
    My God! I'm not ashamed to say
    I cried like a woman there that day;
I was sadder than Thursday of Holy Week,
  For despair and misery.

The only sound was the howl of a cat
   That had stayed by the ruined shack;
      It had made its home in a burrow there,
      And now it crawled from its wretched lair,
When it heard my steps, as if it knew
   It was me, at last come back.

When I left, I'd a bunch of cattle and sheep,
   With my brand on each one of the lot;
      The Justice had said six months at most
      Would be all we'd stay at the frontier post,
And till I came back I left the wife
   In charge of all I'd got.

A neighbour told me afterwards
  That I hadn't been gone very long,
    When they sold the cattle to pay the rent,
    And that after the cattle the land soon went,
And one day the Justice seized the rest
  And auctioned it off for a song.

And my poor boys, when the place broke up,
  Were scattered with the rest;
    They had to go when the land was sold;
    They got jobs as 'peones' I was told,
But how could they work?—the featherless chicks,
  Thrown out too soon from the nest.

When I think of their lot it seems to me
  My heart is near to break.
    They told me the older of the two
    Said he'd stick to the young one, and see him through;
God send some Christian to take them in,
  If only for pity's sake.

And my wife—alas! what good are tears;
  She is lost to me forever.
    They said with some hawk she flew away,
    That had hung round there for many a day;
No doubt she did it to get the bread
  That I wasn't there to give her.

Full often, of things one has to spare,
  Another has none or few;
    When she hadn't a single copper left,
    And of husband and sons she was bereft,
If she wasn't to stay and starve to death,
  What else could the poor thing do?

Alas, dear heart! I fear full sore
 You'll meet no more with me;
  May God keep you in his holy care,
  And cover you, though He leaves me bare,
And here in my song I send my sons,
 My blessing where'er they be.

They were scarcely out of the crib; and now
 They've never a soul to mind them.
  Of their father first they were bereft,
  And now not even their mother's left,
Nor even some faithful dog perhaps,
 Has taken the trail behind them.

Poor wandered waifs without a home,
 Nor a thatch above their heads;
  Perhaps on the open plain they sleep,
  Or into some ruined shack they creep,
With scarcely a shirt to keep them warm,
 Or a poncho for their beds.

Perhaps in want and suffering,
 They wander here and there;
  Perhaps from some cheery blaze, who knows?
  They are driven away with a shower of blows,
And they take themselves off to the plains again,
 In weariness and despair.

And when like a couple of starving curs,
 From the door they're turned away;
  With their tails adroop and their load of woe,
  The two little sons of Fierro go,
To try once more for a kinder door,
 Or into the wilds to stray.

But now in the game I'll take a hand,
　And my all I'll win or lose;
　　My life itself may be the stake,
　　But quarter I'll neither give nor take,
And nobody from this day on,
　Will take me in a noose.

I started soft, but they've made me hard,
　And alone I'll go my way.
　　The rolling plains were all I knew,—
　　The great green earth 'neath the roof of blue,
But I'm bitter now to the bitter world,
　And I know the games men play.

I know the trips and traps and tricks
　That wait for a man in life;
　　I know how they turn and twist and lie,
　　The nets they spread and the knots they tie,
But I'll undo the tangle yet,
　If I do it with my knife.

Let him stand aside who has no call
　To mix in this affray;
　　oOr if not, let him press his hat on tight,
　　And out of these parts, in a hurry, light;
For I'm as mad as a mountain cat
　When they've taken its cubs away.

Though many say that the gaucho is
　An outlaw with scarce a soul,
　　Yet there isn't one, I calculate,
　　But has passed his life at grips with Fate,
Yet he won't give way while the red blood runs
　In his veins and his heart is whole.

VII

ITURNED my back on my ruined home,
But where was I to go?
They called me a tramp, and like a dog
They hounded me to and fro.

When a man is down, I've found it true
That his troubles multiply.
It wasn't long before from the law
I found I had to fly.

I had neither wife nor gear nor shack,
  They called me a runaway;
I hadn't a shirt to cover my back,
  Nor a dollar to pay my way.

I thought I might find my poor lost lads,
  Wherever they might roam,
And together perhaps we'd find us work,
  And I'd make them another home.

But it fell, alas! that all my plans
  Were wrecked by an evil chance;
I heard they were having a spree somewhere,
  And I dropped in to see the dance.

oSo many old friends at the 'pericón'
  I met again that night,
That we all got gay, and I'm sorry to say
  That soon your friend was tight.

I never before, for picking a fight
  Was feeling so inclined,
oWhen a nigger arrived in a swell rig-out
  With a negress up behind.

When the negress got off, I sidled up,
  And I looked at her most polite,
And as she went past I said to her:
  o'It's a little bit . . . chilly to-night.'

She took me up, and to choose her words
  She didn't stop to bother;
For like a flash she answered me:
  'The bigger bitch your mother!'

With a trail like a vixen she bounced inside,
    And rolling her saucer eyes,
And showing a bunch of gleaming teeth,
    Like a mouthful of fresh-cooked maize.

'Good luck, my pretty mare,' said I;
    'My horse has his eye on you';
And leaning against the door I hummed
    A snatch of rhyme I knew:

'God made the white, and Saint Peter the brown,
    At least so I've heard men tell;
But the devil himself he made the black,
    As coals for the fire of hell.'

The nigger was gathering up his rage,
    And was almost ready to bark,
I could see his eyes beginning to glow
    Like lanterns in the dark.

I saw him beginning to paw the ground,—
    I knew how to make him bellow;
I said to him: 'Keep your temper in;
    o'You look like an ass . . . tute fellow.'

The woolly one he gave a jump;
    I could see he was seeing red;
'You're the only ass that's loose to-night,
    You drunken beast,' he said.

And on the word he came in blind,
    And sure would have done me in,
If I hadn't brought him to a stand
    With a whack with the crock of gin.

He gave more grunts than a sucking-pig,
  And he pulled out an ugly knife,
And then with a howl he rushed at me;
  No doubt he wanted my life.

I stepped aside to let him pass,
  And I said to the company:
'Just clear a space please, gentlemen,
  And leave this bull to me.'

The nigger slipped his poncho off,
  For by then he had found his head;
'This bull will be the death of you,
  You gaucho pig,' he said.

While he rolled up his sleeves, I slipped my spurs,
  To be ready for him when he came,
For I had a hunch that the ugly brute
  Might be middling hard to tame.

There's nothing like danger when you're drunk,
  To clear your head, I've found;
Even your eyes get clearer then,
  And things stop going round.

The nigger rushed; and to size him up,
  I let him open the fight;
His first two lunges, with my knife
  I parried left and right.

○I had a 'facón' with an S-shaped guard,
  A blade of the finest kind;
I made a thrust; he threw it off;
  And again he came in blind.

On his fuzzy mop I gave him the flat;
    He let out a terrible roar;
And sprawling and wriggling, down he went,
    Like a squib along the floor.

His wool was all a mat of blood,
    He let out a howl of pain;
○And then like a tigress freshly-pupped,
    He came at me again.

And close in front of my eyes I saw
    His knife-blade wink and flash,
And before I could guard, along my cheek
    He gave me a nasty slash.

At that my blood began to boil,
    As easily you may guess;
And I went for him with point and edge,
    To make one devil the less.

At last with a feint and a side-step quick,
    On my keen knife-point I drew him,
And I lifted him up like a bag of bones,
    And against a fence I threw him.

He kicked and rattled there a bit,
    And twisted himself about,—
I can see him yet,—till like a steer,
    He stiffened his muzzle out.

At that the negress came raging out,
    With her eyes like points of red;
Like a she-wolf there she began to howl
    When she saw her mate was dead.
I had half a mind to give her a whack
    To make her shut her jowl;
But I thought to myself the rest would think
    It was out of place no doubt.
So mostly out of respect for the corpse,
    I left her to howl herself out.

I cleaned my knife on a clump of grass,
    I untethered my nag from the rail;
I took my time to mount, and then,
    At a canter I hit the trail.

They told me they didn't hold a wake,
  Nor over him say a prayer,
But they wrapped him up in a scrap of hide,
  And buried him then and there.

And people tell that since that night,
  By the spot where he was slain,
You will see as you pass an evil light
  That roams like a soul in pain.

And often since then I've had in mind
  To give the poor wretch release,
By dumping his bones in some burying-ground,
  Where perhaps he might rest in peace.

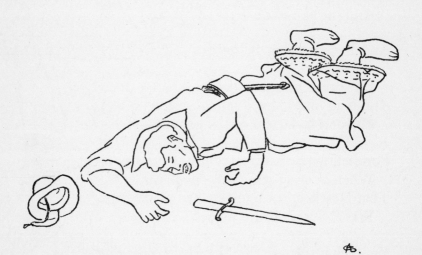

VIII

ANOTHER time, to wet my throat,
  I stopped at a country store,
    When a gaucho famed as a fighting man,
  Came riding up to the door.

oAlmost under the eaves of the porch,
  With a jingle his horse he reined;
While without a word or a look his way,
  At the counter I remained.

He was a bully of thereabouts,
  That did as he liked round there;
He did the Commandant's dirty work,
  And the two went share and share.

And having a big fellow for a
      friend,
  He spread himself all around,
And if anyone crossed him or got in his way,
  He soon had them on the ground.

Poor fellow! he hadn't a doubt, I'm sure,
  When he swaggered into the place,
 That Death, at the game he had won so oft,
  Was about to trump his ace.

Yet such is the way that the world must wag,
  Life deals out weal or woe,
And soon or late, the dice of Fate
  Turn up the losing throw.

He threw himself off, and shouldered aside
  A basque that was by the bar;
    He shoved a half-filled flask at me,
    ∘And 'Drink up, brother-in-law,' said he.—
'By your sister,' I said; 'for in picking her friends,
  Mine's kind of particular.'

'Ah, gaucho!' he said, 'you're a stranger here,
  Or your temper would be more sweet,
    Just up the road there's a burial-yard,
    You must think your hide is thick and hard;
Where this bull bellows there ain't no room
  For a calf to begin to bleat.'

And on the spot like two mad bulls
  Into each other we tore;
    The man was quick, but a bit too rash,
    And a back-hand slash soon settled his hash,
And I left him grunting and thrashing about,
  With his tripes all over the floor.

And as I wasn't at all well in
  With the law of that neighbourhood,
    As soon as I saw him begin to kick,
    I thought I'd better be moving quick;
So I made for the horse-rail, trying to look
  As innocent as I could.

I mounted, and calling on God for help,
  I took up the trail again;
    For the gaucho that gets a bad name must roam,
    There's never a place he can call his home;
Wherever he goes he is dogged by woes,
  And his life is but sorrow and pain.

He is always flying before the law
  In misery, want, and grime;
    He has neither den nor lair nor nest,
    You'd think he was cursed from his mother's breast;
To be a gaucho—that's enough!—
  'Barajo!' that's a crime!

Like an ownerless horse the gaucho is,
  That everyone may ride.
    They break his back and they break his heart,
    For life he must struggle from the start,
Like the tree that without a shelter grows
  On the wind-swept mountain-side.

As soon as he's born and they've baptized him,
  They drop him and give him a whack;
    The priest says: 'You'd better to work begin;
    Run off and find someone to take you in.'
And into the world like a donkey he goes,
  With his suffering on his back.

And here and there with the wind he roams,
  Like a sheep without flock nor fold,
    While his father is pressed by the Government,
    And off to some frontier post is sent;
  No help nor shelter can he get,
    Though he perish of want and cold.

They call him a drunken gaucho beast
  If he takes a spot of gin;
    If he goes to a dance he's an upstart boor;
    If he plays at cards he's a sharper sure;
  He's a brawler if he defends himself;
    If he doesn't—they do him in.

Neither sons nor wife nor friends has he,
  To make his lot less hard.
    He's like a stray bullock that nobody owns,
    And that's only good for its hide and bones;
○For what good is a bullock that doesn't plough,
    Except for the slaughter-yard?

His home is the wild; and his only friends
  Are his lasso, his horse, and knife;
    If dying with hunger and fatigue,
    He drops his loop on some sucking-pig,
  They hunt him off for a 'gaucho-thief,'
    And he has to fly for his life.

And if they stretch him belly-up,
  There's never a soul to care;
    By the side of the trail they let him rot,
    With never a cross to mark the spot,
  Or into some hole, like a dog he's thrown,
    With a curse instead of a prayer.

There's nothing for him in times of peace,
    He's shoved to the front in war;
      If he makes a slip, they don't forgive,
      They think it's enough if they let him live;
  For to fill up his ballot on polling day,
    Is all that they want him for.

In filthy cells and the staking yard,
    One half his life is spent;
      He has no reason, he has no sense,
      If he argues, it's bloody insolence!
     For a wooden bell will sound as well
    As a poor man's argument.

If you plunge and kick, you're a gaucho brute,
    If you don't, you're a gaucho sot;
      Break him up with spurs and quirt!
      Until with his muzzle he ploughs the dirt!
  Of everyone that's a gaucho born,
    This is the mournful lot.

Come then my luck; let's be off together,
    Since together we began.
      Together we must lose or win,
      And stick it out through thick and thin.
  If they bar my path, I will open it up
    With my knife, as befits a man.

IX

SO for many a day I roamed around;
   To a house I never went in;
     I sometimes drew near a ranch by day,
     With my eyes well skinned for a get-away,
In case the police should be hiding there,—
   For I knew they were after my skin.

Like a hunted fox the gaucho lives,
   That has got himself into a scrape,
     Till some day he's off his guard, or rash,
     And the dogs are on him like a flash;
For no matter how well a man can ride,
   From a fall he'll not escape.

At the peaceful hour of the afternoon,
   When everything seems to doze;
     When the winds lie down on the prairie's breast,
     And the whole wide world seems to turn to rest;
To some swamp or brake, with his load of care,
   The homeless gaucho goes.

By the side of the white and woolly sheep,
   The lamb bleats as it goes;
     From the tether-rail the calf calls out
     To the cow that's grazing round about;
But the gaucho has never a friendly ear
   To list to his tale of woes.

So when evening fell I would take me off,
   And some resting-place I found me;
     For where the puma can make its den,
     A man can hide from his fellow-men,
And I knew if they caught me beneath a roof,
   The police would soon surround me.

And although they're only earning their pay,
  And doing their duty no doubt,
    Yet I and they, we don't agree;
    Their law for them, and mine for me;—
And a true-bred gaucho doesn't fight
  Where there's women-folk about.

So all alone on the prairie wide,
  I would wander here and there;
    Sometimes I'd find a ruined shack,
    Or I'd cut some grass to rest my back,
Or lie all night 'neath the open sky,
  oOn some 'vizcacha'-lair.

Between earth and sky on the open plain,
  Without either road or goal,
    Like a lonely ghost, with his load of woes,
    In the darkness the outcast gaucho goes,
And he puts his trust in his prairie-craft,
  To cheat the police patrol.

His prairie-craft and his own stout heart,
  He plays his life upon;
    If he's sore beset and is forced to fly,
    His trusty horse is his sure ally;
No shelter has he but the heaven above,
  No friend but his keen 'facón.'

And just like that on the ground I lay,
  Watching the stars one night,—
    Which it seems to me are finer still,
    When most of sorrows you've got your fill,
So I'd almost swear God set them there
  To mend man's mournful plight.

For there's never a man that rides the plains,
  But holds the stars for friends,
    He's never alone 'neath the star-strewn sky,
    ○Where the 'Three Marias' shine on high;
The twinkling stars are the gaucho's guide,
  When by night o'er the plains he wends.

Here windy words are nothing worth,
  Nor doctors of high degree;
    Here many that think they know a lot,
    Would find their wits tied up in a knot;
For this is a door with a different lock,
  And the gaucho has the key.

'Tis dreary out on the desolate plain
  Alone all night to be;
    To lie awake on the chilly ground,
    And watch the stars of God go round,
With only the silence and the beasts
  To keep one company.

As I've told, one night on the open plain
   I was dozing with one eye skinned,
      While I brooded over my mournful lot,
      When I pricked my ears up like a shot,
∘For from not far off the 'chajá's' call
   Came echoing down the wind.

As flat as a worm I laid me out,
   And I stuck my ear to the ground,
      And soon in the still of the night I caught
      The thud of hoofs at a steady trot.
That they were a tidy bunch I knew,
   For I counted them by the sound.

They seemed to be heading straight my way;
   There was danger, I could feel;
      Not a hair or an eyelash there I stirred,
      And I held my breath until I heard
The creak of leather, the champ of a bit,
   A curse, and a chink of steel.

They were coming so soft that it was plain
   They weren't just taking the air;
      They had tracked me with their dirty spies,
      And were coming to take me by surprise.
It isn't the gaucho's way to run,
   So I started to prepare.

To make a start I crossed myself,
   Then I got out the crock of gin,
      I gave my gizzard a thorough soak,
      For I thought to myself 'If I've got to croak,
To leave good drink for a bunch like that
   Would simply be a sin.'

∘I wound my sash, and I fixed it tight,
My drawers at the knee I tied,
I slipped my spurs, to free my feet,
For I knew I'd have to step quick and neat,
And on a clump of prairie grass
The edge of my knife I tried.

My horse I tethered to the grass,
To have him quick to hand,
I tightened his girth; and to know my ground,
I tried with my foot three paces round;
And then with my back against him there,
I quietly took my stand.

Close up in the dark I heard them rein,
And I thought it time to begin;
I could feel my scalp begin to twitch,—
To get to grips I was all of an itch,—
So I said: 'If you fellows are nursing a grudge,
I'd hate you to hold it in.'

I meant by that to let them know
They were going to find me tough;
I knew that a price was on my head,
And a warrant out, alive or dead,
And of running away from the lousy hounds,
I'd had about just enough.

'You're a gaucho outlaw,' said one of them,
'And we've come to settle your score;
You killed a nigger at a dance,
And a gaucho in a store;

The Sheriff here has a warrant signed
  To lay you in jail to-night;
    And we'll lift your stakes, by the holy Jakes,
      If you're fool enough to fight.'

'Don't come to me,' I said to him,
  'With a lot of dead men's tales;
    The thing we're going to settle now,
      Is if you can get me, and when, and how;
You make me tired with your silly talk
  Of the law, and police, and jails.'

I had scarcely spoke when they tumbled off,
  And all in a heap came on.
    Six paces off they opened out,
      Like a pack of dogs they ringed me about;
I called on the Saints to give me help,
  And I whipped out my 'facón.'

Then close in front of my eyes I saw
  The flash that a musket made;
    But before the fellow could curse his luck
      At missing me, I leapt and struck,—
And as one spits a sardine, there
  I lifted him on my blade.

Another was cramming a bullet down,
  But little it did avail;
    With a single thrust I made him squeal,—
      He no sooner felt the touch of the steel,
Than he gave one jump, and made for home,
  Like a dog when you step on its tail.

They were so cocksure, that to lay their plans
  They had never stopped to worry.
    They tumbled in where I stood at bay,
    And each one got in the other's way;
I got them just as I wanted them,—
  They were blind with rage and hurry.

There were two had swords and were better dressed,
  And that leaders seemed to be;
    ○Their ponchos round their arms they rolled,
    And in front of the others they stepped out bold,
And then like a couple of unslipped hounds,
  Together they rushed at me.

I gave them ground to draw them on
  From the rest of the yelping pack;
    My poncho I trailed,—and when one fool
    Put his foot on it, I gave it a pull;
His heels went up, and down he went,
  Full length upon his back.

When the other one found himself alone,
  He looked a lot less grim.
    I leapt at him ere he fetched his breath,—
    By the length of a knife he missed his death,—
For he turned, and a pair of lifting heels
  Was the last I saw of him.

○One fellow that to a 'tacuara'-cane
  Had lashed a scissor-blade,
    Came rushing in with a flank attack,—
    ○In the dark he looked like a hitching-rack—
I jumped aside and gave him the point,
  And off with a howl he made.

As luck would have it, the dawn just then
    Began to tint the sky,
        And I said to myself: 'If the Virgin now,
        Gets me out of this scrape, I'll take a vow
That from this day on, till the day I die,
    I'll never harm a fly.'

Then into the thick of the lot I leapt,
    While they scattered all around;
        I curled up there like a ball of string,
        With my muscles all set to make my spring,
And in front of two that first came on,
  oI whetted my knife on the ground.

The one that was eagerer of the two,
    Came in with a chop and a thrust;
        I parried once and I parried twice,—
        oIf I hadn't he sure would have killed my lice,
And then before he could come again,
    I filled his eyes with dust.

To follow up I wasn't slow,—
    I was in to him like a flash.
        He hadn't got over his surprise,
        He was rubbing the dust from his blinking eyes,—
'God help you!' I said, and I laid him out
    With a single back-hand slash.

Just then I felt along my ribs,
    A sword-point tap my juice;
        It was only a flesh-cut, I could feel,
        But I went real mad at the touch of steel,
And from that moment among the bunch,
    With a vengeance I cut loose.

The man with the sword nearly had my life
   Before I could prevent him;
     I gave ground quick,—then I firmed my heel,
     And point and edge I gave him steel,—
He twisted his ankle in a pit,
   And to the Pit I sent him.

The heart of a gaucho among them then,
   A Saint must have made rebel;
     Above the rest he shouted loud:
     'God damn your souls for a cowardly crowd!
Before you kill a man like that,
   You'll have to kill Cruz as well!'

And in a jiffy he was afoot,
   And into the fight he sprung.
     I saw my chance, and in I ripped,
     Between us two we had them hipped,
And the fellow Cruz was like a wolf
   When you try to take its young.

The two that faced him he sent to hell
  With thrusts to left and right.
    The ones that were left began to wheel,
    You could see they were sick of the sight of steel;
And when we rushed them they scuttled off
  Like bugs when you strike a light.

o The ones that had stretched their muzzles out,
  All stark and stiff they lay;
    One rode off swaying from side to side,
    While Cruz looked after him and cried:
'You'd better send out some more police
  To cart their dead away.'

I gathered together their remains,
  And I knelt and said a prayer;
    I hunted around for two little sticks,
    To serve the dead for a crucifix,
And then I asked God to forgive my soul
  For killing so many there.

We left the poor fellows in a heap
  Out there on the prairie lone;
    We didn't think it wise to stay—
    I don't know if they were carted away,
o Or whether perhaps the 'caranchos' came
  And picked them bone from bone.

And as we went, between the two
  We passed the crock of gin;
    It's times like that, I always think,
    That make you glad you've saved a drink;
And Cruz, I could see, didn't spare his throat,
  When it came to filling his skin.

We went off trying to sit up straight,
　　But with only half success;
　　　　Our kissing-match with the bottle-neck,
　　　　Till we left it dry, we didn't check;
　　By the way we went stretching our beaks, we looked
　　　Like a couple of storks, I guess.

'I'm off, my friend,' I said to Cruz,
　　'Where Fate may beckon me;
　　　　To stand in my path if anyone dare,
　　　　For a heap of trouble they'd best prepare;
　　For a man is bound to follow his fate,
　　　Whatever his fate may be.

'For many a day my luck's been out,
　　Not a roof can I call my own;
　　　　I'm poorer now than when I commenced,—
　　　　I haven't a post to rub against,
　　Nor a tree to shelter me—little I care,
　　　I can face the world alone.

'Before I left with the army draft,
　　I had cattle and home and wife;
　　　　But when from the frontier I came back,
　　　　All I could find was my ruined shack;
　　God knows my friend, when we'll see the end
　　　Of all this sorrow and strife.'

X

(CRUZ SPEAKS.)

SAID CRUZ: There's never a man, my friend,
But must endure his fate;
And I think the times when all goes wrong,
Are the times for a man to show he's strong,
Until Death cracks him over the head,
As it's bound to, soon or late.

Though I've lost about everything else I had,
I haven't lost my pride,
To be a saint I don't profess,
But I'll help a stranger in a mess;
Though I look like a loaf that's been over-fired,
I'm a cake with a soft inside.

I've had my troubles as well as you,
And no doubt I've myself to blame;
I've stood my share of sufferings,
But they don't count much in my reckonings;
I can put on a limp or a stupid look,
If I find it suits my game.

And so by my wits and a trick or two,
I get my grub and my clothes;
I know when to look like a scabby sheep,
And sometimes you'd think I was half asleep;
But I jump like a glutton for frittered maize,
When the dinner-whistle goes.

I'll say I'm not going to die of grief
  While my pelt is whole and furry.
    Let the sun shine warm in the summer-time,
    Or the winter nip with its bitter rime,—
If this world's a hell, as some men say,
  Then why should a Christian worry?

A hardy front to hardship's brunt,
  Is the surest way to win;
    The craftiest fox that ever laired,
    Like a silly bird at last is snared,
And where he came to lift a lamb,
  On the stakes he leaves his skin.

We've borne the woes that lie behind,
  And there's more no doubt ahead;
    But after all, aren't grief and strife
    The salt and spice of the dish of life?
And in this world man's got to give
  More turns than a bobbin of thread.

It isn't my way to give in to fate,
  Before my fate I meet.
    To know how to fork a colt ain't all,
    ०You've got to know how to take a fall;
And where the gringo breaks his back,
  The gaucho finds his feet.

And it isn't mine, to peak and pine
  O'er the woes of this vale of sorrow;
    I reckon up things like this, my friend,
    That whatever began has got to end;
The day that's gone is yesterday,
  There's another day to-morrow.

I once like you, had a 'china' too,
   And a happy life I passed;
      The days like a peaceful dream unrolled,
      I wouldn't have left for a pot of gold,
If anyone had called me then,
   They'd have found me tethered fast.

The road of love is a broad highway,
   Where none need spur or whip;
      And women know love's every trick,
      And men to learn are apt and quick,
And every gaucho is born to sing
   Of love with a ready lip.

Was ever a man so tough of heart
   That didn't love womenkind?
      Unless a woman's a worthless rake,
      There's nothing she won't do for your sake,
She's the best companion, without a doubt,
   That ever a man can find.

She'll stick to a man through thick and thin,
   Till for good he's down and out;
      Of all his troubles she'll take her share,
      And soothe his pains with her tender care,
  Though you perhaps haven't given her
      A skirt or a ragged clout.

I never so happy was before,
   Nor ever shall be again,
      I was as contented with my lot
      As a fly that lives by a honey-pot;
  La Pucha! my friend, I'll not forget
      How pleasant life was then.

She was the song-bird that lighted down
   From the sky on the lonely tree,
      She was as fair as the dawn of day,
      When the plain is gold with the sun's first ray,
  She was the flower that scents the wind
      On the clover-covered lea.

But soon the Commandante there,
   Who was head of the Army post,
      Began to loiter around my place,—
      There was trouble writ in his ugly face,—
  And of slipping in when I was away,
      Not a chance the rascal lost.

He was always calling me his friend,
   But little I liked his look;
      His word was law all round about,
      When he came I could hardly turn him out,
  ○And soon in my 'rancho' he was stuck
     ○As firm as a liver-fluke.

It wasn't long before I guessed
  That he had unseated me.
    He went about with his tail in the air,
    And he took to sending me here and there
With some fool message for excuse,
  And without even thanks for fee.

And now and then for nothing at all,
  Whenever his whim might suit,
    To some town or ranch I'd have to go,
    That would keep me away for a day or so,
While never in his Commandancy,
  He as much as set his foot.

A worse mischance to any man
  There scarcely can befall,
    Than to have to pass his lonely life
    Without the help of a faithful wife;
But to keep a woman for someone else,—
  Far better have none at all.

It ruffles me up when another cock
  Comes crowing around my yard.
    For many a day I nursed my sore,
    Till I made up my mind I'd stand no more;
And messing with her beside the fire,
  I caught him off his guard.

The dirty old rascal had a face
  ○Like a fresh-born half-licked calf.
    When I saw the way he was making free,
    I tell you it only disgusted me.
'You must have been starved for a bit of love,'
  I said to him with a laugh.

He pulled his sword and made a jump,
  And to jab at me began;
    I saw he was nearly blue with funk,—
    It wasn't worth while to kill the skunk—
So I said, 'If you wait you'll bog yourself;
  Hitch a trace, and get out while you can.'

He made a couple of aimless thrusts,
  And squeaked like a cornered rat;
    I stepped aside from his point, and then,
    As I make it a rule not to kill old men,
I pulled my 'facón,' and not too hard,
  oI gave him a whack with the flat.

But as a boss is never short
  Of some hang-dog follower,
    A fellow there when he heard the fuss,
    Rushed in on me fair venomous,—
He jumped through the doorway gritting his teeth,
  And snarling like a cur.

oHe popped at me with a fancy gun
   That had six shots in the barrel;
      He meant to get me, it was clear,
      I felt the bullet singe my ear,—
It's lucky for me I get nimbler-kneed,
   The deeper I'm in a quarrel.

He went on loosing his shots at me,
   Till I began to get mad at the fellow.
      I tell you he made me duck and dance,
      Till I saw my opening, and took a chance,—
Then in I jumped, and I ripped him up
   Without giving him time to bellow.

When I'd finished with him, to find his boss
   I hunted left and right;
      He had hidden himself in a tub of lye,
      He made me laugh till I thought I'd die,
He was slimed all over from head to foot,
   And nearly dead with fright.

By hell!—The Christian male's a fool,
   When love leads him a dance;—
      oHe looked at her, and his eyes went stiff . . .
      And I suddenly caught such a terrible whiff!
That on the spot, like a startled horse,
   For the door I began to prance.

I said: 'You've played a losing game;
   What you've dropped is your own affair!'
      I didn't want another dose,
      So I went off sneezing and holding my nose,
And like a kid that's sick with worms,
   I left him snuffling there.

Now as a rule, a backing mule,
　Is a mule that's about to kick;
　　And a woman that backs has got no cure,
　　The same as a mule, she'll hoof you sure;
When you see her start to paw around,
　It's a sign to be moving quick.

So all by the fault of a flighty jade,
　That wanted to fool two men,
　　I took my poncho and my things,
　　And hit the trail with my sufferings,
And I said good-bye to the cosy home
　That never I'd see again.

And since that day I've never again
　With women tried my luck.
　　It's only a fool his wits will back
　　Against loaded dice or a pin-marked pack;
A woman or a fresh-pupped bitch,
　With neither will I have truck.

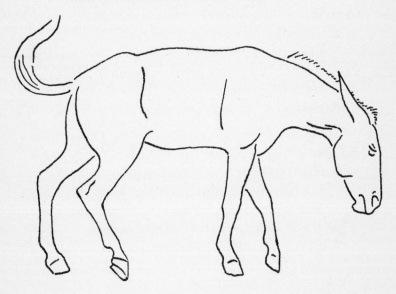

XI

WHEN others sing—like a bubbling spring
    The couplets out may gush;
       And although my verses poor may be,
       It's more or less the same with me,
For my rhymes leap out like a flock of sheep,
    When out of the pen they rush.

For scarce the first one clears the gate,
    Than out the next one pops;
       Against the bars the others heap,
       And struggle and jostle and press and leap,
And till the last of the flock is out,
    The stampede never stops.

And though I've never been to school,
    And books are to me a puzzle,
       I can mend with will, what I'm short in skill,
       And once I'm in form and open my bill,
As soon as one verse gets out of the gate,
    Another one shows its muzzle.

So lend you ears to me, my friend,
    And I'll tell you my tale of pains.
       My life has been nothing but grief and woe,
       And what else is false,—I've found this so:
That the gaucho pays for his ignorance,
    With the life-blood of his veins.

After that stroke of evil chance,
  To the scrub-lands off I went,
    Like a hunted beast without a lair,
    For weeks I lay in hiding there;
I got my food as best I could,
  And a terrible time I spent.

And so much of hunger and wretchedness,
  And sorrows of every sort,
    I had to bear while they hunted me,
    That I nearly gave in, from misery,
And I almost think my heart since then,
  Has hardened to a wart.

The hue and cry began to die,
  But that didn't end my woes,
    One day I heard, by evil chance,
    That not far off they were holding a dance,
And for the 'pulpería' straight
  I turned my horse's nose.

The place where they'd fixed to hold the dance
  Was an evil-looking shack;
    It filled up so you could scarce get in,
    And soon some tempers were wearing thin;
When a poor man wants to enjoy himself,
  Of trouble there's never lack.

I had a pair of half-boots on,
  All covered with boils and weals;
    They had a ridge along the hock
    That looked like the spurs of a fighting-cock;
It made me worried to look at them,
For I thought I had corns on my heels.

oWith 'gato' and 'fandango' there,
   The frolic they begun;
     I hadn't danced for many a day,
     So in I slipped to the party gay,
But the Devil put his tail in the game,
   And messed up all the fun.

A wall-eyed gaucho, hard of mouth,
   Was playing the guitar.
     I never was good at holding my hand,
     And I know what I should or shouldn't stand,
And if anyone starts to look for me,
   La Pucha! he won't look far.

I led a filly out to dance
The 'pericón' with me.
As soon as the fellow saw me there,
He knew who I was,—for I saw him stare;
And he sang these rhymes in the worst of taste,
As I think you will agree.

o'Women are hard to drive
As a mule,
And they're flighty too
As a rule;
They'll fly and leave a man,
Like a fool.

Woman and vicious horse,
Beware you gall;
Better ride slow and sure,
Than not at all;
Rash riders soon or late,
Ride for a fall.'

At that the women all cleared out,
And I twisted upon my heel;
I shouted: 'Cricket,—shut your row!
If you're looking for trouble, have it now!'
And like a flash, with a sounding crash,
I sliced his strings with my steel.

Then out at a door a gringo jumped
With a gun, to join the fight.
But all my life I've been hard to scare,
And I know all the tricks, and some to spare . . .
In a jiffy I slipped my poncho off,
And threw it over the light.

I yelled 'Stand clear if you love your lives!'
　　With a leap I gained the door;
　　　　The dancers were all mixed up in the dark,
　　　　And some of the men took the chance for a lark—
And with curses and howls and yells for help
　　The place was all in a roar.

The singer first came tumbling out,
　　And straight he rushed at me;
　　　　But when I'm in trouble I don't lose touch,
　　　　Though I may have drunk a glass too much;
And at handling the knife, by some I'm held
　　As middling quick to be.

There was nothing could better have suited me.
　　I made him pay dear for his wit.
　　　　I was ready for him; for as I've said,
　　　　There's nothing like fighting clears my head;
I lifted him up on the point of my knife,
　　Like a pigeon on a spit.

There's always women at hand to help
　　A man in his sufferings.
　　　　Against some tubs they propped him up,
　　　　The while he howled like a mangled pup;
He was showing enough of his guts to make
　　A brand new set of strings.

I mounted and made for the open plain,
　　As free as the winds that roam;
　　　　Like the clouds that race o'er the heaven's face,
　　　　And know neither halt nor abiding-place,
The outlawed gaucho has no rest,
　　And can call no place his home.

And the lot heaven sends to every man,
   Each man must bear it through;
      If a thing's just so, then why complain?
      You don't cut hide against the grain;
When we scratch ourselves, we all scratch up,
   It is our nature to.

For the slightest slip that the gaucho makes,
   To the wilderness he's driven,
      To make his home with the ostriches,
      While others with more advantages,
No matter what crimes they are guilty of,
   They'll always be forgiven.

XII

I LOST my count of the weary months,
That wretched life I led.
   At times we were so short of food,
   That some stray horse we barbecued,—
I had banded up with some others there,
   That from the law had fled.

But why complain? We must play our lives
   With the cards that Chance has dealt.
      The gaucho is born,—and old he grows,
      But the passing years never mend his woes,
Until some day Fate nooses him,
   And Death collects his pelt.

Yet no matter how long a trouble lasts,
   It's bound to have an end.
      And so at length it happened to me,
      That I got relief from my misery
For with the Judge my affair was fixed
   By the help of a mutual friend.

I must tell you there's scarcely a gaucho left
   All round my native parts;
      Some are under the grass, and some have fled,
      And some in the frontier wars are dead;
For as soon, in this land, as one war is done,
   Some other rumpus starts.

And it seems to me that that was why
   The Justice of the Peace,
      As soon from the warrant as I was free,
      Sent along to say that he wanted me;
And he told me he'd give me a job with him,
   As a soldier in the Police.

'A fine brave fellow' he said I was,
    In a flowery rigmarole.
       I got—as the gist of his long harangue—
       That he wanted me to join his gang,
And that I was a Sergeant from that day on,
    And head of the Police patrol.

So that's how I came to be doing a job
    I never had no heart in;
       Last night when he sent us to take you there,
       I saw at once we're a well-matched pair;
And it's little I like to go blunting steel
    In quarrels I have no part in.

       .   .   .   .   .   .

I've told you my story now, my friend;
    And I guess our fates agree.
       The man Cruz gives his hand as friend,
       As sure as himself can on Cruz depend;
As a comrade true, I'll trail with you,
    If you'll throw in your lot with me.

Then it's ho! for a wild and roving life,—
    No fear but with grit and wit,
       We'll ever lack on the open track,
       A colt to back or a bottle to smack,
A grassy couch on the rolling plain,
    ∘And a strip off the ribs for the spit.

And when with the wear of time and chance,
    Scarce a rag to our backs is left,
       I'll ask some wolf to lend me his skin,
       And when I've cured it and beat it thin,
It'll do for a poncho supple and warm,
    And as soft as the finest weft.

For me the spine is a juicy steak,
　　And the tail as good as the breast;
　　　　I can sleep wherever I happen to be,
　　　　And eat whatever God sends to me;
　　I can fight like a bull, or act the lamb,
　　Whichever may suit me best.

Let the ball of fate go rolling on,
　　It'll come to a stop some day;
　　　　The gaucho's life is a struggle grim,
　　　　Till Death takes his legs from under him;
oOr we get a 'criollo' Government,
　　That rules in the gaucho way.

For the wretched gaucho they care as much
　　As the scraps one throws the dogs;
　　　　They treat him harsh, with an iron hand,
　　　　And seeing it's them as has command,
We must just put up with Fortune's stripes,
　　However hard she flogs.

La Pucha! if you could have only heard
　　The talk I heard one night!
　　　　When one of them came to talk to the Judge;
　　　　I was just outside and I didn't budge;
I tell you, my friend, my hair stood up,
　　And my heart curled up with fright.

They were full of a plan for getting rich
　　With the pick of the frontier lands;
　　　　And as far as I could catch their drift,
　　　　The frontier itself they were going to shift,
And press in men from far and wide,
　　To chase out the Indian bands.

I never heard such a mass of schemes,
  Nor so many tricks in one bag;
    They'd say there was millions had to be spent,
    And swindle it all from the Government,
While us poor soldiers—the bloody swine!
  They grudge us a bean or a rag!

And if things go on as up to now,
  Our troubles may soon be done;
    For our wretched lot 'tis little they care,
    They'll plunder the land till they leave it bare,
With only a litter of dead men's bones
  To whiten in the sun.

On the bucking back of Fortune's jade,
  The gaucho's doomed to sit.
    He never arrives, though he travels hard,
    And once they catch him off his guard,
They lift him up at the end of a noose,
  Without leaving him time to spit.

    The townsmen talk of the gaucho's woes,
      And the wrongs we suffer under;
        ○But they're up to the 'tero's' trick, I'll
        swear,
        To save their own nests is all they care;
    They kick up a shindy over here,
      But their eggs are over yonder.

    They fiddle around with their knife in the neck,
      And let on they can't find the throttle;
        They send out a Justice of the Peace,
        With a long pay-roll for more police;
    But to cure the gaucho's bellyache,
      They've made a mistake in the bottle.

A.

XIII

(MARTIN FIERRO SPEAKS.)

WE'RE chips, said I, of the self-same block,—
We'd might as well match our plans;
I'm a gaucho that's got an evil name
And more or less you're much the same;
And as for me—to end this mess,
I'm off to the Indians.

I trust that God who so oft before
His mercy has shown to me,
If I do wrong now, will my sins forgive,
While with the heathen I've got to live;
If I'm cruel to those who were cruel to me,
I but follow my destiny.

God fashioned the flowers of the plain,
In a hundred colours dressed,
He made them delicate and fair,
He gave them beauty and to spare,
But more than the flowers he gave to man,
When he put a heart in his breast.

God gave its brightness to the light,
He gave strength to the wind,
He gave the eagle's wing its flight,
And even the ant he gave its sight;
But he gave much more when he gave to man
An understanding mind.

God taught the birds of the air the songs,
They sing with their little beaks,
He gave them their shining feathers too,
And a lot more things; but to me and you,
He gave much more than he gave the birds,
When he gave us a tongue that speaks.

And since to the savage beasts he gave
Their rage and violence,
That no one can tame, and nothing fright;
When he made us men, he thought it right,
To give us wit, and courage too,
To serve for our defence.

And so many good things all at once,
He gave him, that I suppose,
He figured it out that the human breed
The whole of those benefits would need,
To make the balance level up
Against their load of woes.

And out of this hell I think it's time
For good and all I went.
I'm pretty tough; I can handle a lance,
With the Indians I'll take my chance;
We'll be better off when we get outside
The reach of the Government.

In the hunting-lands of the Indians,
    Where there's neither law nor jail,
        They'll take you into their brotherhood,
        If you deal with them as a Christian should;
I'm tired of living on the run,—
    It's me for the frontier trail!

There's perils enough along the way,
    And trials and sufferings sore;
        But danger never yet frightened me,
        And things are just what they've got to be;
If we miss the way, there's many a one
    Has missed the way before.

And whether we keep, or lose our lives,
    It's little that men will care;
        We only need to keep going west,
        And leave it to God to do the rest;
We'll arrive some day; and afterwards,
    Time enough to find out where.

And I'll tell you, pard; the way's not hard,
    For two such well-matched twins.
        Though where he starts from he doesn't know,
        The gaucho heads where he wants to go,
o As the withered grass-blades bend their tips
    To the side where the day begins.

We needn't fear we'll starve to death
    In the desolate wilderness;
        If you're not too dainty about your meat,
        There's lots of beasts that are good to eat,
o 'Matacos,' and 'quirquinchos' too,
    And 'mulitas' and ostriches.

What you catch in the desert you gobble up,
　　And scarce leave bones or skin.
　　　They say even women have come safe through;
　　　And it will be—I warrant you—
　○A gaucho ostrich that gets away,
　　○When my 'Three Marias' spin.

We may feel thirsty now and then,
　　But that doesn't worry me;
　　　I don't mind going dry for a day,
　　　I can smell a river miles away,
I can tell when there's water at the root
　　Of the 'duraznillo' tree.

We'll be more safe with the savages
　　Than ever we have been here.
　　　We'll say good-bye to our sufferings,
　　　And you'll see high jinks and junketings,
The day we drop in to some Indian camp,
　　Beyond the far frontier.

We'll make a tent to hold us both,
　　And we'll live luxurious;
　　　With a few horse hides it's easily done,
　　　A parlour and kitchen all in one,
And it may be some 'china' will pity our lot,
　　And come and keep house for us.

You don't need to do a stroke of work,
　　Your board and lodging's found;
　　　In a raid now and then you'll do your share,—
　　　If you come back sound that's all you care;
And the rest of the time you lie belly-up
　　Just watching the sun go round.

Our luck's been nought but a fickle jade,
    That's played us fast and loose;
        Let's throw her over for good, my friend,
        And perhaps of our troubles we'll see the end;
For every land is a brave man's home—
    Let's be off, amigo Cruz.

A man that can handle the 'bolas' well,
    And rope a running steer,
        And sit out the jolt of a bucking colt,
        When it clears the gate like a thunderbolt,—
Of finding a home with the savages,
    Need never have a fear.

With a song on his lips the gaucho loves,
   With a song he draws his knife;
      We'll live as well over there as here,
      And in the raids we can get us gear;
And to finish a story that's long enough,—
   I'm done with this wandering life.

.   .   .   .   .   .

When he got to this point the singer stopped,
   And grabbed for the liquor jar;
      Straight up to heaven he tipped his chin,
      And when he had sluiced his pipes with gin,—
On the ground with a crash, at a single bash,
   He shivered his guitar.

'Lie there,' he said to the instrument;
   'Don't tempt your master more;
      I'll not have another twang your strings,
      And fondle you, while his songs he sings,
Nor ever another shall take up
   The song that here is o'er.'

And now before I close my rhyme,
   For my story is almost through—
      There's some that like women go off real vexed
      Unless you tell them what happened next;
So if they listen, I'll round the tale
   Before I take leave of you.

Well, Cruz and Fierro cut out a troop
   From one of the ranges near;
      With a sleek bell-mare to lead the string,
      They had no fear of them scattering,—
And driving the troop ahead of them,
   They made for the far frontier.

And then one day, when the sun's first ray
  Made the plain like a sheet of gold;
    Cruz pointed back where the eye scarce caught
    The last ranch stand like a tiny dot,
And as he looked, two burning tears
  Down the cheeks of Fierro rolled.

And then they struck the desert trail,
  And passed beyond my ken.
    I've never known if their goal they made;
    If they lived, or were killed in some Indian raid,
But I trust that some day not far away,
  I'll have word of them again.

And here my friends, my story ends,
And so my rhyme I'll close.
Remember this: what I've told to you,
From beginning to end is gospel-true,
And that every gaucho that you meet
Is a bundle of pains and woes.

Put your trust in God who made us all,
And cares for the suffering;
With this I now my tale conclude,
Since I've told to you as best I could,
The wrongs that all of us have to bear,
But that I've been the first to sing.

THE END OF THE FIRST PART

THE GAUCHO
MARTIN FIERRO

Part the Second

THE RETURN
OF MARTIN FIERRO

I

Introduction

NOW lend your ears to me, my friends,
   And let your tongues be dumb;
     And if my memory serves me well,
     I'll sing again of what me befell,
And I'll show you now that of my tale
   The best was still to come.

When out of the world a man comes back
   To mix with his fellow-men,
     He's half asleep and his eyes are dim,
     And their faces all seem strange to him,
But perhaps the sound of the thrumming strings
   Will wake up my wits again.

It's so mighty long, since I sang a song
   That I scarce know how to start;
     But bear with me till I find the note,
     And the song will come, and I'll loose my throat,
And the souls of singers dead and gone
   Will strengthen my lips and heart.

oIf the deal doesn't give me thirty-one,
   With thirty I can't go wrong,
     I haven't a doubt I'll scoop the pool;
     As a brat I sang before I could pule;
When they christened me, instead of howls
   I let out a burst of song.

Before I'm done, both rich and poor
　　To listen I shall compel.
　　　　I haven't a doubt, if they hear me out,
　　　　They'll stay to admire where they came to flout;
And though I may make them laugh a bit,
　oThey'll have to weep as well.

They've lots to tell who have suffered long
　　The bite of sorrow's tooth;
　　　　And to make a start I'll ask you here,
　　　　To take on trust what you may think queer;
When a man isn't paid to tell a lie,
　　It's odds that he tells the truth.

To the Holy Virgin I give thanks,
　　And praise to God in heaven,
　　　　That 'mid all the pains and suffering sore,
　　　　The losses and hardships that I bore,
I kept my voice and the power of song,
　　That at birth to me was given.

That every living thing should sing,
　　The Father of all ordains;
　　　　There's never a creature with a voice,
　　　　That doesn't with song its heart rejoice;
The voice is the song of the rich red blood
　　That swells in the throbbing veins.

If a townsman sings—he's a poet born—
　　But a gaucho!—he's crazed or tight;
　　　　Like an ostrich flock they stand and gaze,
　　　　At his ignorance they're all amaze.—
But even the darkness has its use
　　The better to see the light.

They call the plainsman a stupid boor,
    And they put on uppish looks;
        But I on the plains who was born and bred,
        I'll tell them this:—when all is said,
They'll find in my song if they listen well
    More sense than in lots of books.

O many singers have I known
    That it was a joy to hear;
        But little they cared for right or wrong,
        If the song was sweet, they sang the song,
But little care I what ears I jar,
    If I make my meaning clear.

The singer that takes this way must bring
    All his wit and skill along,
        And altho' my knowledge and craft be small,
        The heart is what matters after all,
And the proof is not if the song be sweet,
    But the sense behind the song.

The pictures I'm going to paint will last
    For men not born to scan,
        I don't need any to show me how,
        Or change my drawing, then or now,
The man doesn't paint who would like to paint,
    But the man, I guess, that can.

Yet I'd have you know it's not for show
    That here I sing my best;
        Though of telling the truth I've never been sorry,
        There's some home-truths stir up lots of worry,
And to say some things too loud and plain,
    Is to stir up a hornet's nest.

But along this path that I choose to go,
    I'll take my way alone;
        I ask no favour of anyone,
        I fear no man and I flatter none,
And I'll sing no tale that I heard or dreamt
    But of what I've seen and known.

And if anyone wants to take me up,
    He will have to know a lot,
        And a lot he'll learn who listens well,
        To the tale that here I've come to tell;
And lots of you will have cud to chew,
    Before to the end I've got.

When you that listen and I who sing
    Are dust in the wind of years,
        My songs in remembrance men will keep,
        As long as they labour and fight and weep;
I've chewed tough meat to make this brag,
    And salted it well with tears.

There's a sigh astir in my heaving breast,
    And a sob within my rhyme.
        For of want and sorrow and pain and woe,
        There's never another has suffered so,
And to blot my tale out of memory,
    I challenge the hand of Time.

But soon you'll see if you bear with me,
    How I'll wake up more and more,
        And once I'm warm it won't be long
        Ere I give its head to the rolling song,
And don't be surprised if I sing in a key
    That you haven't heard before.

And with every tautened cord a-ring
  I'll sing as of old I sang;
    We'll sing a match my guitar and I,
    And we won't give in till my throat goes dry,
Or I lose my voice, or the stops give way
  Or the strings themselves go bang.

Though I smashed my guitar last time I sang,
  And I haven't sung since that day,
    When the heart is full the song will out,
    And I've got such things to sing about,
That God forbid he should ever bear
  Who taught me first to play.

And nobody bade me here to sing
  And nobody chose my song;
    I'll sing what I want to, last and first,
    What I can't keep in, if I'm not to burst,
And it's up to the man who sings this way,
  To sing out clear and strong.

For many a year I've followed my luck
  And I've nought but scars to show,
    And now from the wilds I've turned again
    To live once more with my fellow men,
To see if they'll let me live in peace,
  And work at the things I know.

I can rope on foot a running steer
  Though it comes like a thunderbolt;
    I can ride in the round-up, part and brand;
    In the corral too I'm a first rate hand;
○I can sit as firm on a wagon-shaft
  As I can on a bucking colt.

Then gather around and I'll thank you well,
  If you listen well to me;
    Yet if you won't, it's little I care,
    I'll take myself off some other where;
For the song-bird never stays for long
  When it lights on a flowerless tree.

There's many a clout to be shaken out,
  And dust to be raised up too;
    Just settle down and clear your wit,
    And let me unbuckle myself a bit,
I'm so well primed that once I start
  You'll have to hear me through.

But before I go on just pass the crock,
  And give me a swig of gin,
    My pipes seem dry, so I won't be shy,
    I'm not ashamed if I drink, not I,
If you want to keep up the singer's fire,
  You've got to put fuel in.

II

MARTIN FIERRO RELATES HIS TRAVELS IN
THE DESERT

WITH a mournful note my strings resound,
And the matter suits it so;
No merry tale to you I sing,
But the toils and troubles and suffering
Of one who was born, grows old, and dies
In a round of unbroken woe.

It's sad to leave one's native parts
   To roam in an unknown land,
      With one's heart bowed down with a load of care,
      And no home or refuge anywhere,
Hurled on by Fate, as the desert wind
   Hurls on the lifted sand.

To take one's way without guide or goal
   O'er the trackless wilderness,
      Like an outlaw cast from the haunts of men,
      And to leave behind, as we did then,
The wife one loves and one's little sons,
   God knows in what sore distress.

Ah, how often there on that mighty plain
   Where the days creep by like years,
      The shapes of the past in our minds would rise
      And a mist would gather before our eyes,
Till we threw ourselves down in some clump of scrub
   And solaced our grief with tears.

I mind me once by a little stream
   In the shade of a stunted tree,
      I grieved alone o'er the times long-fled,
      And it seemed whenever I turned my head
That I caught a glimpse of my 'china's' form,
   And heard her calling me.

And gulp by gulp from a sky-blue pool
   My horse there drank his fill,
      While gulp by gulp my throat went dry
      And my breast heaved many a bitter sigh,
As I thought of my home and my wife and sons
   That haunted my memory still.

You'll remember maybe, how Cruz and me
    Crossed the line one golden dawn,
        And side by side o'er the Pampa wide
        With only the sun and the stars for guide,
We rode till we came to an Indian camp,
    The first we had chanced upon.

But alas for our hopes! our luck was out,
    By a hair we missed our death;
        The Caciques were holding a talking match,
        The plot of a murderous raid to hatch;
And at times like that those heathen brutes
    Distrust their very breath.

The fat was in the fire before
    We could think about retreat;
        I never heard such a dreadful din
        As their howling horde came closing in,
And athirst for blood they swooped on us
    Like flies on fresh-killed meat.

They took us for spies and in a trice,
    They snatched our mounts away,
        Some jabbered to kill us out of hand,
        Each wanted his way; there was no command,
An inch from our eyes their lances flashed
    And I thought it was time to pray.

They leapt and yelled while above their heads
    A forest of spears they shook,
        And one of them span his bolas there
        So close to my head that they ruffled my hair,
I thought we had not a minute to live
    Except by a lucky fluke.

The only thing in his savage creed
   That the Indian's sure about
      Is this; that it's always good to kill,
      And of smoking blood to drink his fill;
And the blood he can't drink when his belly's full
   He likes to see bubble out.

Said Cruz, 'Old pard; tho' to die is hard
   It's fighting I like it best;
      Let's teach them the feel of the gaucho steel.'
      'Hold on,' said I, 'till the thing's past heal';
Of danger the man is least afraid
   That has faced it oftenest.

The worse the quarrel you're landed in
   The more you'll find caution good;
      You'll come off best if you keep your head
      When the other fellow's seeing red;
And to keep cool blood behind your blade
   Takes nothing from hardihood.

At last a parleyer came to say
   We could keep our skins just then;
      'A cacique has saved your lives,' he said,
      'Since you're worth much more alive than dead;
Our plans are all laid for a mighty raid
   On the curséd Christian men.'

'And he's told the rest till the raid is done
   As hostages you'll do;
      In case some brave of the raiding band,
      Should fall alive to the Christians' hand,
We can hold your blood for their blood in fee;
   And ransom them with you.'

With that they fell to their talk again
   To finish their hellish plan,
      In a ring they reined their horses round
      And planted their spear-butts on the ground;
Along the line on the lances points
   The sun-beams winked and ran.

In the middle the oldest of the lot
   Began to rant and roar.
      He loosed them a terrible rigmarole,
      And believe it or not, upon my soul,
He made that gang stick his long harangue,
   A good three hours and more.

At last three horrible howls he gave
   And they broke with a devilish din—
      To master his horse is the Indian's pride,
      There's few of us ride as he can ride;
He'll rein at full tilt to a sliding stand
   Then round like a top he'll spin.

In a ring anew their mounts they drew
   A-rein with plunge and prance,
      While the old cacique reviewed the lot
      And gave each a howl as a parting shot,
And every howl he drove well home
   With a shake of his quivering lance.

And soon the whole plain began to boil,
   The din was worse than a battle;
      Indians and horses and dust and yells
      Like the fury loosed from a hundred hells,
It made the flesh on your bones to shake
   And your very bones to rattle.

When the Indian's blood is fired to kill
    He's worse than a savage beast;
        With streaming hair and lance in air
        They raced and wheeled like a whirlwind there;
    Before the hullabaloo died down,
        Was a couple of hours at least.

It was little sleep that night we got
    For our nerves were all on edge;
        To kill our hopes of a breakaway
        They ringed us round till the dawn of day,
    And to double our fears they planted spears
        All round us like a hedge.

And a sentinel they placed as well
    To watch us like an owl;
        When we thought the horde was all a-snore
        o'Huincá' at random one would roar,
    And from every Satan's son would come
        'Huincá!' the answering howl!

But nevertheless at other times
    The Indian's a sluggish brute;
        He sleeps like lead as if he was dead,
        You'd think his snores would burst his head,
    If the world should crack beneath his back
        He wouldn't stir hand or foot.

They started to ask us a hundred things,
    They wanted to know a lot;
        When the Indian raids he takes good care
        To know what force is mustered there,
    And the kind they are and who orders them,
        And the horses and arms they've got.

And at every answer we gave to them
  One would throw back his head and yell;
    And like a shot, the whole bang lot
    Would take to roaring on the spot
'Huincá! huincá!' again and again,
  Like devils a-howl in hell.

When all together they make their roar,
  It starts like a far-off drum,
    And little by little it rises high,
    Till it seems to fill all the earth and sky—
The terrible cry of the Indian horde
  That strikes the Christians numb.

III

HE RELATES HIS LIFE AMONG THE INDIANS

SO there were we—friend Cruz and me
   With our lives in the lap of Fate;
     But even when trouble has got you grassed
    You must keep up your pecker till the last;
If a man keeps thinking about his death
   He may think of his life too late.

There's nothing on earth a man can't face
   Nor the heart need be afraid;
     We knew for the worst we'd best prepare
    So we swore an oath between us there
We'd bow to nought save the will of God;
   Then for help to Him we prayed.

Misfortune is like a hardy tree
   When you lop it, it sprouts again;
     If you're born of a woman beneath the sun,
    Be you wise or foolish—every one
Gets his share of grief, even mother earth
   Bears venom as well as grain.

It's a wise man's part to bear his ills
   Without complaint or pother;
     For myself, I butt up against pain and woe
    Whatever I do and wherever I go;
Ill-luck begets crops of ugly brats
   Though she seem to have had no mother.

Go far, go fast, man meets at last
  The fate that with him was born;
    No matter how much he may think he can,
    He'll not escape from Destiny's plan;
If you handle a thistle it stings because
  That's why it was given its thorn.

The poor man's life is a struggle grim,
  Of trouble he'll never lack,
    Like the hungry kite he must keep awake,
    For want comes swift and it knows no slake,
If the bitter blast of misfortune's wind
  Some day unroofs his shack.

But though God sends woe, some comfort too
  By His grace in grief is found;
    Though the sun doesn't bother its beams to aim
    They light on each one of us just the same,
And even the very thinnest hair
  Throws its shadow on the ground.

No matter if hardship flogs your back
  Or sorrow wrings your eyes,
    Remember this that I tell to you;
    Keep your backbone straight and you'll yet win
      through,
The straightest and proudest tree that grows
  Is the poplar—that always sighs. . . .

When the Indian isn't making a raid
  He lives in a brutish style,
    On his well-filled belly he lies all day
    No law but the lance he will obey,
And like a beast what he lacks in brains
  He makes up in distrust and guile.

If you ever should find, an Indian kind,
  You may put him in a show;
    The captives that fall to the infidel
    Would fare as well mid the fiends in hell;
For pity's not even a word to him,
  And he never forgives his foe.

It is useless to hope for favours there
  Or for clemency to pray.
    Out of sheer mistrust of what we might do
    They parted us after a day or two,
And an Indian guard kept watch and ward
  Beside each of us night and day.

Though to roam a little for scraps of food
　　At times they let us loose,
　　　　To change a word we'd never a chance
　　　　For they'd drive us back with yell and lance,
So through two long years we dragged our lives
　　In loneliness, me and Cruz.

It would lengthen the tale to no avail
　　To tell all the ills we bore;
　　　　So I'll only say that there came a day
　　　　They sent to take our guards away,
And we heard with joy that the chief had said
　　We could be together once more.

A little way off was a belt of scrub
　　And we pitched our shelter there;
　　　　To rig us a tent they gave us leave
　　　　With two horse-hides; at morn and eve
∘It looked to me like two tilted hands
　　With the fingers joined in prayer.

To that tiny nook our rags we took
　　In misery there to dwell.
　　　　It was some relief to be on our own,
　　　　And better together than each alone;
Yet sad we were as a burial ground
　　At the sound of the funeral bell.

The man who would roam must take out from home
　　Stout heart and a hide that's thick;
　　　　When he's on the trail they'll stand him true
　　　　When he pitches camp he'll need them too,
He must back his life on his ready knife,
　　Or he'll get his quietus quick.

A calf that's hungry's a calf that's tame,
   And it sucks from any cow;
     The gaucho knows what hunger is,
     And he'll sympathize with our miseries,
I tell you we scoured and scavenged for food,
   Without caring what, when, or how.

Long hours we spent in our little tent,
   And many a crack we had;
     In the vermin-wars we were veterans,
     They worried us less than the Indians;
We were lean and tough and they got just enough
   To keep them fighting-mad.

There's never a brute, when you hunt on foot
   But's got a good get-away,
     You've got to be sly and sure and spry
     And quick as a flash, of hand and eye,
And always close to the water's edge
   Like a beaver you've got to stay.

When you live like that not the mountain cat
   To hunt has a keener wit;
     It doesn't matter what beast it be,
     oFrom fat 'peludo' to bird in tree—
Every beast that burrows or walks or flies,
   Is fellow-well-met with the spit.

We hunted north and we hunted south
   We hunted east and west;
     We were up and away with the dawning light
     And seldom got back before the night,
We scoured the plains and the hollows and hills
   And poked every burrow and nest.

If you live by the hunt it won't be long
    Till you lose your squeamish taste;
        Fur or feather or shell or scale,
        The speck that moves you'll be on its trail,
And roast or raw it will glut your maw
    And never a bit you'll waste.

The Master of All, both great and small
    Is God in His holy heaven;
        He teaches each beast to hunt its food
        And to leave the bad and to take the good;
And he sees to it that to each of them
    Its proper meat is given.

There's a different meat for each beast to eat
    If it fly or swim or run;
        But it's strange to see how the tribe of man
        Doesn't fit quite into that common plan,
He's the only beast that can laugh and weep,
    And he gobbles up every one.

IV

RAIDS OF THE INDIANS

AT the faintest ray of the breaking day
   The Indian begins to stir,
      And oft in the night they were up and gone,
      Before we knew that a raid was on;
And when dawn was pale they were far on the trail,
   To pillage and massacre.

Before they go off, in holes and caves
   Their goods and gear they dump;
      They don't take a thing but what they need,
      They ride bare-back on their wiry steed,
And all they wear is their matted hair,
   And a rag tied round their rump.

From his string of mounts the Indian takes
   The fleetest and surest-paced,
      And—the deadliest arm on the open plain—
      His long, keen lance of sturdy cane,
And two or three pairs of 'bolas' too
   He fastens at his waist.

They travel light, for day and night,
   With scarce a halt they ride,
      They wear a spur when they're on a raid,
      From the sharpened tip of a deer's horn made,
Behind their ankle they fix it fast
   Tied on with a strip of hide.

The Indian that owns a horse
   That's out of the common run,
      He waits on that animal hand and foot,
      There's nothing he won't do for the brute,
And he hires it out to some raiding brave,
   Until the raid is done.

He'll see it's fed when of food himself
   He's scarce got a single thing;
      To watch it many a nap he'll miss;
      He's a sloven in every thing but this.
By night he makes his family sleep
   All round it in a ring.

As you'll have seen if you've ever been
   In a running frontier fight,
      And if you haven't, remember well
      That every single infidel,
Rides a horse picked out of a hundred score
   That can run like a streak of light.

The Indian's pace is an easy lope,
   The pace that a horse can stay;
      You'll never find him roam around,
      With his head for his goal he eats the ground,
Not a single beast on the darkest night
   When he hunts can get away.

Without losing touch they form a line
   And a night-long drive commence;
      Far out ahead the ends they fling,
      Till the points join up and close the ring.
At dawn there's game to pick and choose
   As safe as inside a fence.

A pillar of smoke is the sign they use
　　To bid the tribes come in;
　　　　For miles and miles the signal's seen,
　　　　It rises high and their eyes are keen,
And little by little the muster swells
　　And louder grows the din.

And that's the way they gather there
　　Those horrible howling bands
　　　　That fall like a swarm on town and farm;
　　　　Before the Christian has time to arm,
They have seen the sign; they have sniffed the wind
　　And they come like the desert sands. . . .

The Indian's war is a desperate war,
No savage beast is worse;
Of looting and killing he never tires,
The ruins he leaves behind, he fires;
He puts his faith in his murderous lance
And his fleet and wiry horse.

oIf you wait for him, take in your belt
As soon as you hear his howls,
To the tiger-cat if you make your plea
For pity, you'll get it more easily;
The Indian's heart is a bag of bile,
And there's iron in his bowels.

He never spares; like the fiend he hates
All Christians to the death;
And it isn't alone when he's fighting-mad,
When his blood is cool he's just as bad,
For pity's dart never stings his heart
And cruelty's his very breath.

oFrom the puma he gets his reckless rage,
From the eagle he gets his sight;
In the grassy plains or the desert sands
Every beast that lives he understands,
And he learns from each what it has to teach
Of cruelty, craft, and fight.

From birth to death the Indian's blood
Like a boiling torrent flows,
A single spark in his savage mind
Of brotherhood don't hope to find,
To fight and kill and to drink his fill,
Are the only joys he knows.

The Indian grins and shows his teeth
  oBut to laugh he never can;
    When he comes from a raid he will jump and shout
    And twist his eyes and lips about,
But to show his joy with a smile or a laugh
  Is the mark of the Christian.

  Like ravening beasts on the scent of blood
    They come o'er the desert broad,
      Their terrible cries fill the earth and skies
      And make every hair on your head to rise,
  Every mother's son of their howling horde
    Seems a devil damned by God.

All the work the Indian ever does
  He leaves to his women folks,
    It's quite enough if he fights and drinks,
    Of anything else he never thinks;
An Indian thief the brute was born
  And an Indian thief he croaks.

They dip their arms in a poison-brew
  That their filthy witches make;
    They fear neither Book, nor bell, nor ban,
    Nor the wrath of God nor the rage of man;
From the savage brutes of their native wilds
  oTheir barbarous names they take.

And Christ! At the thought of their filthy ways
  The wind in my nose grows rank;
    All higgledy-piggledy piled inside
    Of their stinking tents of putrid hide,
Men, brutes, and women, and bugs, and brats
  In their dirt they stewed and stank.

If you haven't seen it you won't believe,
If you have you'll not forget—
    The sloth and want that there we saw;
    The Indian recks not Adam's law
That the earth will only bear her fruit
    Where the tiller drops his sweat.

V

RETURN FROM A RAID AND DISTRIBUTION OF BOOTY

THE desert boils when with their spoils
The raiding bands come in;
They drive the cattle on before,
In a cloud of dust o'er the plain they pour,
If your heart doesn't sadden at the sight
It must have a good hard skin.

The whole place seethes with beasts and men
Like grains in a brimming bin,
And when the last of the herds they round
The tramp of their hoofs fair shakes the ground,
From brim to brim the plain is choked,
No eye can take them in.

It's the women's job, the goods they rob
　　To bring back from the raid.
　　　　It makes one sad to see the packs
　　　　Of pillage piled on the horses' backs,
The looted goods of the Christian's homes,
　　And the frontier shopman's trade.

It's plunder they're after first and last
　　When they ravage the Christian's land;
　　　　There's nothing they meet doesn't stuff their bag,
　　　　They don't leave even the dead a rag,
If they don't make off with the Government
　　It's because it's not to hand. . . .

When they've all come in they there begin
　　To divide the plunder quick,
　　　　And soon—as the 'santiagueños' say—
　　　　○The 'repartija' is under way;
They jumble it all up in a heap
　　And nobody gets his pick.

And on the spot they divide the lot
　　And they dole out share and share.
　　　　It's a ticklish job, but they don't discuss:
　　　　Each takes his whack without any fuss,
It's the only time that you'll ever see
　　The Indian on the square.

And when in their tents they've dumped their loot
　　They take the plain again;
　　　　And like demons there the livelong day
　　　　The crowded beasts they slay and slay,
Till the plain as far as the eye can see
　　Is piled like a slaughter-pen.

And when with blood he has slaked his rage,
　　And there's nothing left to kill,
　　　He throws himself down like a lazy brute
　　　And hardly will move a hand or foot,
○While the women come with their skinning knives
　　And fall to work with a will.

A few tag-ends of the herd sometimes
　　They'll drive to the hinterland,
　　　But there's few of them will trouble or dare
　　　To try to trade with them over there,
For as like as not they lose the lot
　　To some other Indian band.

But of all the tribes of that barbarous brood
　　The Pampa is hard to beat;
　　　Though to cover their fud they've only a clout
　　　And there's scarce a thing they don't go without,
A hundred cows they will kill for sport
　　For one that they sell or eat.

Worse things than these for years I've seen
　　That the hardiest might appal;
　　　But time brings changes as the years move on
　　　And the days of the mighty raids are gone,
And the Indian's power has had its hour
　　And is checked for good and all.

The tribes are harried and scattered far,
　　Their day is almost done;
　　　The chiefs that a thousand lances led,
　　　Are captives now, or long since dead;
And lancer and looter stand at bay
　　In the glow of the setting sun.

The Indian is savage through and through,
　　He seems like a thing accurst;
　　　　For even in sport he's a cruel brute
　　　　And cruel to his kith and kin to boot,
　　And that's where the women play their part,
　　And the women come off worst.

By the way that a man treats women folk
　　You can measure him to a tee;
　　　　For myself, I don't think the world's worth while
　　　　Without the light of a woman's smile;
　　The man that can win a woman's love
　　Is the happy man for me.

And every man that can read life's plan;
　　His joy in her love will find;
　　　　And it's only fit that the strong man's arm
　　　　Should be her fence against hurt or harm;
　　It's only the man with a craven's heart
　　That is rough with his woman-kind.

To help a man when he takes a fall
　　From the bucking jade of fate,
　　　　There's always some woman standing by
　　　　And there's never a danger makes her fly,
　　There isn't a woman born, I think,
　　That isn't compassionate.

　　There isn't a woman in all the world
　　　　That doesn't feel pity's dart.
　　　　　　For woman I thank God's holy grace,
　　　　　　But not because of her pretty face,
　　　　But because in each woman that walks the earth
　　　　He planted a mother's heart.

She's godlier far than we men are
　　In her tasks she'll never flag,
　　　　Perhaps I don't praise her half enough—
　　　　My words seem poor and my voice gets gruff—
Yet the Indian treats his women worse
　　Than a scrap of filthy rag.

He makes her toil from morn to night
　　In a round of drudgery;
　　　　He masters her like an animal,
　　　　She's always at his beck and call,
For even in love his stony heart
　　Doesn't lose its cruelty.

For parent or friend or child or wife
　　He cares not a single straw,
　　　　His brutish heart none may hope to win,
　　　　His breast is bronze outside and in,
I measured them up that day we came,
　　When their devil's pranks I saw.

Those years we spent in our little tent,
　　I had time his ways to mark;
　　　　The Indian's belly's his only god
　　　　He's the greediest beast above the sod,
○At the sight of food he's like the crow
　　That forgot to come back to the Ark.

As soon as wink, on a crucifix
　　He'll spit, or his foot he'll set;
　　　　The cat for rage, and the pig for sloth,
　　　　The Indian outdoes them both,
And man and brute they eat the fruit
　　That their own loins beget.

A hundred tales of their evil ways
　I could tell of the Indians,
　　Forgive me please if I've left the track,
　　To my story's trail I'll now get back;
　And I'll tell you the sort of savage sport
　　That delights the barbarians.

　　　　.　　.　　.　　.　　.　　.

Their spears they take, and a hedge they make
　Firm planted in the ground,
　　The braves crowd round to watch the show,
　　And into the ring the women go.—
Like a troop of mares on the threshing floor,
　oThey make them go round and round.

They start the romp with all state and pomp,
　The chiefs make a dress parade;
　　With horn and pipe and sheepskin drum
　　They fair raise pandemonium,
While round and round inside the fence
　Not a moment the dance is stayed.

Far over the plain at times one hears
　The hounded women's wail;
　　But most often the sound in the din is drowned
　　While all around that circus-ground,
The drunken Indians lie and howl
　Like beasts on a blooded trail.

A single word that they never change,
　From start to end they yell;
　　Together they howl, while the time they beat
　　With heads and bodies and hands and feet,
o'Ioká!—Ioká!'—I can see them yet
　As ugly as imps from hell.

And all night long they make them run
  Inside that trampled pen;
    Starving and weary and soaked with sweat
    They goad them on with prod and threat;
  Though it thunder and pour, 'Ioká!' they roar,
'Ioká!' and 'Ioká!' again.

VI

CRUZ

THE days rolled on and months crept by
  While in hopeless plight we pined;
    Yet one of the chiefs of the Indian band
    That had kept them from killing us out of hand,
Tho' he kept aloof, gave us sometimes proof,
  That his heart was a different kind.

A noble heart that savage had
  A Christian he longed to be,
    It's only just he should have his due,
    He used to give us a horse or two,
And once or twice he slipped away
  And visited Cruz and me.

I quarrel not with whatever lot
  God sends, be it joy or pain,
    Yet often and often I thought, ah! Christ!
    We had bought our lives too dearly priced;
And I wished we had never seen that chief,
  But been by the Indians slain.

The blessings and boons man gets in life
  It hoves him not forget,
    But when to the kicks of Fate you roll
    There's many a pang you'll have to thole,
And by many a scrape and scathe and scape
  You'll find the trail beset.

And slowly here I'm drawing near
   To the saddest of the tale,
     At the memory of a bitter cup
     It's a bitter thing again to sup;—
The small-pox broke on the savages
   Like a storm of poisoned hail.

Like fiends possest by a demon guest
   'Neath the pelt of the leaping sore,
     'Gualicho! Gualicho!' went up the yell:
     'The Christians cast the Gualicho spell.'
And like a herd of maddened beasts
   The tents were all a-roar.

Their remedies are the sorceries
   That their witches know alone;
     Their 'chinas' can't cure the sick or hurt,
     But some old hag thick-caked with dirt,
Stands by while they put the sick man through
   The spells of the filthy crone.

The patient there has got to bear
   A hail of whacks and thumps;
     They fall on him and they pound and squeeze,
     And knead him well with their fists and knees,
They pummel and kick and they punch and prick
   And they tear out his hair in clumps.

A thousand pains they serve him there
   Each worse than the other one,
     The Indian roars like a bull that's grassed
     But he can't get away for they truss him fast,
And to finish they grease him from head to foot
   And put him to boil in the sun.

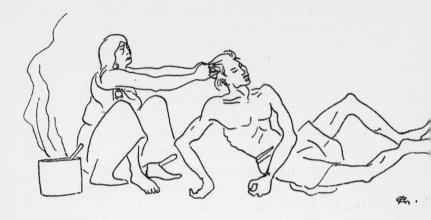

And when he's stretched out muzzle-up
   Some more of their tricks they try;
      They build a fire all round him near,
      And a woman howls in the wretch's ear;
If any get better, it seems to me
   It's because they're too damned to die.

At other times they burn their mouths
   Though they squirm and squirm again,
      They wring their limbs with twist and turn
      While their lips and teeth and gums they burn
With a scalding egg from the witch's pot
   That was laid by a spell-bound hen.

The Indian knows what's in store for him
   From the moment he feels him sick;
      He runs like a hare if he gets the chance
      For it's kill or cure, between witch and lance;
If with fever or dread he goes off his head
   They finish him good and quick.

The fever they take, it makes them shake
    Till they're terrible to see.
        I'll leave to others the hows and whys,
        But it wouldn't cause me much surprise
If their fevers are worse from eating horse,
    For that's how it seems to me.

A captive they had, a gringo lad
    That babbled of ships and docks,
        Like a little blue pony's were his eyes,
        The limpid blue of the prairie skies,—
In a muddy puddle they drowned the boy
    As the cause of that plague of pox.

A haggard old witch gave the word to kill,
    And they rushed at him in a heap,
        Though he struggled and cried in his despair,
        To stones he might better have made his prayer,
His eyes turned round till they showed the whites,
    Like the eyes of a dying sheep.

As far as we dared we moved our tent,
    For the havoc shook our hearts.
        To add to our terror and dismay,
        Cruz felt the fever himself one day,
And desperate then we laid our plans
    To make for our native parts.

But the best laid plans of mice and men
    Full oft they go agley;
        When I think of it my blood runs cold:
        The chief that had saved us as I've told,
Was stricken sore the day before
    We had meant to go away.

The pestilence grim had its grip on him,
He was soaked with the fever sweat;
When we saw his state we had never a doubt
It was only time till his light went out;
Cruz turned to me, and 'Old pard,' said he,
'Here's a chance to pay our debt.'

We couldn't do less than stop, I guess,
So we scrapped the plans we'd laid;
And when they came to drag him out
To beat him and burn and maul him about;
We managed to save him from witch or lance,
And firm in his tent we stayed.

And fiercer still the black-pox raged,
The Indians died like flies;
We did what we could for our stricken friend.
We watched in turns to the bitter end,
But few days passed ere he breathed his last;
With a prayer Cruz closed his eyes.

And then alas! my grief's renewed
When I open my memory's store,
From my eyes the bitter tear-drops start
And an icy chill creeps round my heart,—
My comrade Cruz by the loathsome plague
Was smit, to rise no more.

What grief was mine you may well divine
When I saw his end was near;
All helpless there I saw him lie
And inch by inch I watched him die,
While not even a prayer I could call to mind
To comfort his dying ear.

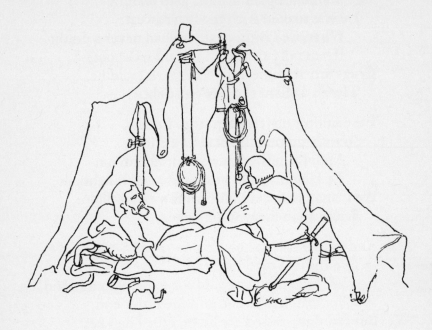

O'er his breast and head the foul pest spread,
   His life was a long-drawn groan;
      He said to me: 'Martin, old friend:
      I'm getting out to my tether's end;
There's my boy, back home,—you'll look for him:
   When I'm gone he'll be all alone.

'If you ever get quit of this quag we've hit,
   You'll look for my wandered foal,
      There was only two of us, me and him,
      Since his mother went—but things get dim—
Just tell him how his father died—
   And to God commend my soul.'

Against my breast his head I pressed,
  I was crazed and blind with sorrow.
    He fretted sore, I can understand,
    To die in the midst of that heathen band,
And there in my arms he hit the trail,
  For the land of the Great To-morrow.

I called on Jesus to take his soul,
  And a stammered prayer I said;
    I felt his limbs grow stiff and stark,
    And before my eyes the day went dark,
And I felt as one struck by a thunderbolt
  When I saw Cruz lying dead.

VII

THE WAILS IN THE DESERT

IN my arms he died, that comrade tried,
His like I shall ne'er possess,
    His nerves were steel and his heart was gold,
    He was true and steady and wise and bold,
To pay a debt to a savage foe
    He died in the wilderness.

On the sun-baked plain I dug his grave,
    With my hands I heaped the sod,
        My heart was full to the bitter brim,
        The soil was wet where I buried him
As I knelt by the head of his narrow bed
    And prayed for his soul to God.

No rite or office I left undone
    Though my soul was sick with loss;
        With trembling hands I cut two sticks,
        And as best I could, made a crucifix;
And there in the wild I left my friend
    Asleep 'neath that little cross.

From tent to tent with my grief I went,
    The Indians let me be;
        I was reckless then of what might befall,
        The world was sour and my life was gall,
And to and fro wherever I'd go,
    I could hear Cruz calling me.

Every man that's born in this troubled land
  Is more or less cured to woe;
    But by day or night for my aching heart
    No cure I could find, for all my art,
Except on the ground by Cruz's grave
  My desolate breast to throw.

And there by the grave of that comrade brave
  I would lie for hours on end,
    With my breast and brow on his couch of sod
    And none to watch but Almighty God,
And I'd groan and sigh for the days gone by,
  Home, wife, and sons and friend.

I was stripped like a bone of all my own,
  Forlorn in a savage land;
    The wheels of time grief seemed to clog,
    Like a waggon fast in a dreary bog,
Till it seemed some days on my woes to gaze
  The sun would stock-still stand.

As here and there in my deep despair
  I roamed to no avail,
    One day on the plain, out of sight or sound
    Of the Indian's scattered camping-ground,
The wind to my ears of a sudden blew
  The sound of a bitter wail.

It's no surprise to hear groans and cries
  In the tents of that heathen brood;
    For yonder it's only wild-beast law—
    The gnashing fang and the ripping claw—
And everything's fixed with the knife and lance
  And the bolas and hardihood.

No traveller's oath need Fierro take,
  But his simple words believe:
    A savage I've seen take a tiny maid
    And cut her throat with a dagger-blade,
And out of the tent her mangled corpse
  To the dogs like offal heave.

I've seen many killings out of hand,
  And some killed bit by bit.
    I've seen some horrors that have no name,
    And cruelties that the beasts would shame,
For neither the Indian nor his dam
  For mercy care one whit.

I pricked my ears when I heard the cries,
   I listened a bit, and then,
      I crept up softly, keeping low
      To find out the cause of those sounds of woe;
The hair on my head still bristles up
   When I picture that scene again.

A wretched woman was crouching there
   At the feet of an Indian;
      Like a Magdalen her tears ran down,
      She was spattered with blood from sole to crown,
Like the stab of a lance, I knew at a glance,
   That she was a Christian.

As softly then as the mountain cat,
   Keeping cover, I crept along,
      For the Pampa savage trusts no man,
      Save the devilish brood of his own foul clan,
He held in his grip a cattle whip
   Blood-soaked both butt and thong.

VIII

THE CAPTIVE TELLS FIERRO HER STORY

THE evil fate that had brought her there
  She later told to me:
    One day like a storm the Indians came,
    Her home went up in smoke and flame,
  They killed her man and brought her back
  To their tents a slave to be.—

In a hopeless round of racking toil
  Two years had passed away;
    Her little son they had let her keep,
    A little chick that scarce could cheep;
  The Indian's woman hated her
  And hounded her night and day.

She had waited in vain for a chance to fly
  And take to the trackless plain;
    For a dead man's woman the posts don't stir,
    There's ransom for others, but not for her;
  A captive there she ends her days,
  In misery, filth and pain.

That Indian's mate in her savage hate
  Made her life a round of pain,
    She glutted her pride on her white-skinned slave,
    Her man was a haughty Indian brave,
  He wore round his neck a string of teeth
  From the Christians he had slain.

That evil woman would put her to work
  With her child close by her side;
    In the chilly morn while the light was pale
    On the ground she left it to shiver and wail,
Like a trussed-up lamb its hands and feet,
  With a leather thong she tied.

She would set her a long and heavy task
  That the strongest arm might test,
    At gathering wood or sowing corn,
    While her little one cried out all forlorn,
Till her task was finished she didn't get leave
  To give it her mother-breast.

When of work there was lack for her arms or back
  To some other she lent her out;
    'There's none,' she said, 'would ever believe,
    The evil tricks that their hearts conceive;
What a woman captive has to bear
  One doesn't dare think about.'

If she has a son and the boy grows up,
  As no pity they understand,
    And prayers for mercy they never heed,
    They take him away though she weep and plead
And they sell him or barter him for a horse
  To some other Indian band.

The Indian woman's cruel enough
  To her own little wretched brat;
    On a piece of wood she keeps it bound,
    With rags she swathes it round and round,
And there it'll stay for many a day
  oTill the back of its head gets flat.

Though it may seem queer, I tell you here
  It's the stamp of their barbarous kind;
    It's nothing more than the sober truth,
    The Indian admires what we think uncouth
And he's proud as Punch if his cranium
  Sticks up in a point behind.

There was never sate to the 'china's' hate
  As the weary months went by;
    Till at last when her sister died one day,
    All round the tents she began to say
The Christian woman had worked her death
  By the spell of the Evil Eye.

On the plain the Indian dragged her out
  And first with threats he tried
    To make that Christian woman tell
    By what evil arts she had cast the spell,
He threatened to flog her like a dog
  Till under the lash she died.

While he stormed and raved, through her blinding tears
  For mercy she prayed in vain;
    Her little one in her arms she pressed
    But he tore it away from the sheltering breast,
And with the first stroke of the raw-hide thong
  He made her writhe with pain.

And that savage there her quivering flesh
  Like a fiend began to thrash;
    The blows rained thick on her back and head,
    He raved like a beast as the thong grew red,
While with arms and hands she tried to stave
  The beat of the whirling lash.

Until at length with a back-hand blow
  He felled her with the butt
     And howling out: 'So you won't confess?'
     To crown the cup of her bitterness
He plucked her baby from where it lay
  And its throat at her feet he cut.

'It doesn't seem true,' the poor thing said,
  'There are demons in human guise;
     It might drive any mother raving mad—
     Not a spark of compassion yon Indian had,—
In cold stark hate that innocent babe
  He butchered before my eyes.'

At those horrors the Christian's curdling blood
    Almost stops through his veins to run;—
      'That merciless savage,' she said to me
      While she shook with sobs at the memory,
'Tied my hands together—the cord
    Was the bowels of my little son.'

IX

MARTIN FIERRO'S FIGHT WITH THE INDIAN

THE wails I had followed up were hers,
As she writhed 'neath the pitiless lash;
The whole foul scene at a glance I took,—
I didn't need a second look,—
And the part that there it was mine to play
I knew like a lightning flash.

The wretched victim bathed in blood
At the Indian's feet I saw,
The raw-hide thong from head to heel
Had left its mark in welt and weal,
And through the rents of her tattered dress
The flesh showed red and raw.

To heaven there in dumb despair
She raised her streaming eyes;
From her wrists the ghastly tether hung,
My heart like a twisted clout was wrung,
She gave me a look that called for help
More strong than a hundred cries.

Shall I tell in a song how the angered blood
Through my tingling pulses stirred?
The Indian turned and our eye-beams clashed,
From eye to eye the challenge flashed,
We knew each other man to man
And we wasted never a word.

With the backward leap of the cornered cat
　　His fighting length he chose,
　　　　He watched me there like a beast at bay
　　　　That knows it must either be slain or slay,
　　His 'bolas' from his belt he loosed
　　And waited for me to close.

Though it wasn't to look for trouble that day
　　That out on the plain I'd gone,
　　　　I tied my reins, from my horse I slipped,
　　　　From its sheath my trusty steel I whipped
ₒThat never needs loading or misses fire
　　And the fight was up and on.

I knew the mouthful I'd bitten off
　　Was going to be tough to chew;
　　　　We watched each other with all our eyes,
　　　　Not a chance we gave for a quick surprise,
　　But each of us waited warily
　　To see what his foe would do.

When the Indian crouches, peel your eyes
　　And don't dare even wink;
　　　　If you do, you'll scarcely get off alive,
　　　　Like that he's as good as four or five,
　　With a puma's bound he leaves the ground
　　And he gets you before you think.

I couldn't trust to a reckless rush,
　　It was death to beat retreat;
　　　　And worse than either it was to wait.
　　　　The fix I was in was desperate;
　　For more might come, and among the lot
　　I'd soon be butcher's meat.

There's many a time I've saved my hide
   By dint of taking care;
      When a man in a risky fix is fast
      The slightest slip may be his last,
I wouldn't have worried half as much
   If Cruz had been only there.

When a man's got a partner in a fight
   He's double as bold and strong;
      He cares not a rap for trick or trap
      And Cruz was a glutton in a scrap;
The two of us could have taken on
   The tribe if they'd come along!

That somebody there was about to die
   Was as plain as plain could be;
      There wasn't much choice what I had to do,
      There was no way out, but one of two:
To stiffen that son of Satan out,
   Before he could stiffen me.

But time was passing, the matter urged,
   I had to do something soon;
      As his chance he seemed content to bide,
      With a sidling step I moved aside,
As if I was going to grab his horse,
   And wish him good afternoon.

He fell for that, and he didn't wait,
   With a howl he leapt for me;
      There's nothing worse to the Indian brute,
      Than to lose his horse and be left afoot,
And when he rushes,—neat and quick
   On your feet you've got to be.

He lashed the air with two 'bola' shots,
  Round his head like rings they spun;
    One grazed my arm with a glancing hit,
    A hair's breadth more would have splintered it;
  Those balls of stone whizz through the air
    Like bullets from a gun.

When my opening pass with the knife I tried
  He curled up rump to heel;
    In all my travels I've never met
    Such a bag of tricks as that savage yet;
  And I've never seen one half so spry
    To get out of the way of steel.

A terror he was with the 'bolas' too,
  Like streaks from his hand they sped;
    He gathered them in like a jiffy there
    And again they'd whistle through the air,
  My heart kept jumping up my throat
    As they whizzed above my head.

Aijuna! I'll say he was quick and sly—
  He missed me by simple luck;
    The blood worked up to his ugly head,
    Till like a colt he was seeing red:
  He would feint at me with the right hand ball
    Before with the left he struck.

But a bitter turn Fate served me there
  As we circled round and round,
    I saw my chance and went rushing in,
    While he backed away to save his skin,
  My foot tripped up in my 'chiripá'
    And headlong I hit the ground.

Not a moment's grace to commend my soul
　　To the hands of Almighty God
　　　　Did the savage give; as he saw me fall
　　　　He sprang like a ravening animal,
　　As I twisted my head, beside my ear
　　　I heard the 'bolas' thud.

And onto my back with tooth and nail
　　He leapt like a clawing brute
　　　　He was reckless then that I'd still my knife,
　　　　He was blind with his rage to have my life,
　　Not a ghost of a chance he let me have,
　　　To straighten and get my foot.

No trick or dodge could the brute dislodge
　　Though I tried them every one;
　　　　Flat under him I lay full length,
　　　　I couldn't turn over with all my strength,
　　As strong as a bull that Indian was
　　　And he seemed to weigh a ton.

　　　　·　　·　　·　　·　　·

Ah gracious Father of all that lives,
　　Who can read your ways or plan?
　　　　When a woman's arm in that bitter hour
　　　　You clad in a flash with magic power,
　　And her tender heart you moved to deeds
　　　More bold than many a man.

The captive that lay in her tears and blood
　　Half killed by the murderous whip,
　　　　When she saw my plight forgot her pang,
　　　　Like an arrow there to my help she sprang,
　　She gave the Indian a sudden tug
　　　That made him lose his grip.

From the deadly clasp of the Indian's grasp
   That woman set me free,
      A moment more I'd have been past cure,
      Without her help, he'd have croaked me sure;
My heart swelled up to twice its size
   When I saw what she dared for me.

As soon as again to my feet I got
   At each other again we tore,
      Not a pause for a breather could I get
      I was soaking wet with my dripping sweat,
In all my fights I'd never been in
   Such a touch-and-go before.

Not a moment either I gave him rest
   As you may well suppose,
      As time slipped by my cares increased
      For fear with his 'bolas' the vengeful beast
Might brain the woman, if I paused,
   With one of his lightning blows.

The 'bolas' in an Indian's hands
   Are lumps of flying death;
      Like streaks around his head they spin
      While like a goat he leaps out and in,
Like beasts we fought and in word or cry
   We wasted no single breath.

As long as I live I'll not forget
   That duel in the wilderness;
      The stake of the strife was death or life,
      The Indian's 'bolas' against my knife,
And for watcher there of our desperate game,
   A woman in sore distress.

As madder and madder the savage grew
 I calmed down more and more,—
  Until the Indian has made his kill
  There's nothing his ravening rage can still,—
Till one of his whirling cords I cut
 And began to press him sore.

My ribs he rang with a 'bola' shot—
 A dozen more went wild—
  Then I saw my chance and with stab and hack
  I went for him—the brute stepped back
And by fate or luck his heels he struck
 On the corpse of the butchered child.

I'll leave to wits more wise than mine
 What I don't understand—
  It seemed to me as he backward trod,
  He was tripped by the wrath of Almighty God;
Where chance isn't present you'll often find
 That Providence takes a hand.

As he staggered back, I leapt and closed
  With lightning thrust and slash,
    Though he kept his feet and escaped my grip
    He lost the fight by that fateful slip;
I got home once with a scalping-chop
  And once with a belly-gash.

When he felt the wounds he was less cocksure,
  And began to drop his jowl,
    But he was an Indian as tough as made,
    Though his blood ran out his courage stayed,
And back he came, while from his throat
  He let out howl on howl.

From the chop I had fetched him on the head
  The blood mussed up his sight,
    From his other wound, as we circled round,
    It splashed in puddles on the ground,
Though he felt it splatter about his feet
  He wouldn't give up the fight.

Three terrible figures there we made
  In that fight with the infidel;
    The mother knelt and her hands she wrung,
    There was me, all in, with my lolling tongue,
And the savage there like a foam-flecked beast
  Spewed out of the depths of hell.

The Indian felt that the horn for him
  Was sounding the slaughter-blast,
    His hair stood up and his eyes rolled round,
    He was staggering now on the trampled ground,
He sucked his lips in out of sight
  As his breath came thick and fast.

I got him again with a ripping lunge,
  He began to humph and puke;
    He was failing fast with each breath he took,
    He knew he was done, but even then,
    With never a flinch he rushed again,
With such a yell that it seemed to me
  That the earth and the heavens shook.

And there, thank God, I finished him;
  Well home I rammed my knife.
    I was weary and sore, but desperate,
    I lifted him up as one lifts a weight;
And gutted there, from the raking steel
I threw him off when I knew by the feel,
  That he hadn't a spark of life.

When I saw him dead I crossed myself,
  The help of heaven to thank;
    The kneeling woman beside me there,
    At the Indian's body could only stare,
And then to the skies she raised her eyes,
  And in tears on the ground she sank.

On the boundless plain by that woman's side,
  With the great blue sky above,
    I knelt and gave thanks to my patron Saint,
    While she to God's Mother made her plaint;
Through her sobs she prayed for both of us
  To the Holy Virgin's love.

And slowly then, like a lioness
   Despoiled of her only pup,
      While her tears still ran in a blinding flood,
      All soaked in blood, from the trampled mud,
   She picked the limbs of her mangled child,
      That I helped her to gather up.

THE RETURN OF MARTIN FIERRO

THERE was nothing for it after that
  Than to fly from the Indian's land.
    Though I'd killed the brave in open fight,
      They wouldn't argue the wrong or right,
  As soon as they found his body there
  They'd lance me out of hand.

I mounted the woman on my horse,
  From the tether I set him free;
    A mount was that of the finest breed,
    A stayer, and speedy too at need,
  When I whistled, wherever he was he came
  And rubbed his nose on me.

McCook Community College

There isn't a danger in all the world
   But mounted well, I'll meet;
      The Indian's horse was a glossy black,
      I was fit for anything on its back,
It could cover the ground like a leaping hound
   oWith the 'bolas' round its feet.

There was nothing it met on the open plain
   That worried it in its stride;
      The Indians teach them to run like light
      Till they run down an ostrich flock in flight,
oAnd throw the 'bolas' from under the neck
   As stretched on the ribs they ride.

To train his mount for the hand-to-hand
   Is the Pampa warrior's pride,
      He is off at a pat of the Indian's hand,
      In the length of a stride he'll come to stand;
At a twitch of the rein like a top he spins
   In the space of a bullock's hide.

Every day as soon as the sun is up
   His paces he puts him through;
      He trains him to run where the going's rough
      On the moving sand and the bog and bluff,
If you look for a horse that's better trained
   You'll find there's mighty few.

When you're forking a mount that's Indian trained
   You needn't fear a roll,
      La Pucha! and as for doing a bolt
      There's none can outpace or outlast his colt,
He doesn't tame it with quirt and spur
   oBut with word-and-hand control.

He handles it softly for a start,
Its neck with his hand he slicks,
He doesn't care what time he'll spend,
He strokes it there for hours on end,
And he only stops when it drops its ears
And neither jibs nor kicks.

Not a single blow he gives it there
With whip or yet with hand;
There's no patienter thing in the universe
Than the way of an Indian with a horse,
When he's finished with it his every word
The beast can understand.

Though at breaking a colt in our Christian style
I don't waste sentiment,
It's better I like the Indian way,
And the horse, once rid, the very next day,
You'll see with the reins across his neck
At the flap of the Indian's tent.

If you want a horse that's a model mount
　From the Indian take this tip;
　　Don't beat him up till he goes to bits,
　　Just treat him soft till the brute submits,
If he takes a fall don't drag at his mouth
　And savage him with the whip.

There's lots of busters with whip and spur
　That boast of the breaker's art,
　　But a big raw brute with a vicious eye,
　　They'll always leave until by and by,
Or they'll tie him up to a snubbing post
　Until they've broke his heart.

They're ready with reasons of every sort,
　It's 'but' and 'perhaps' and 'if';
　　It's best to prepare him a bit, they say,
　　They'll put him through it some other day,
But a fool can see with half an eye
　The beast has scared them stiff.

The animal of the horse's kind
　(Forgive me these indications)
　　Has touchy feelings and lots of sense,
　　It's easy to get its confidence,
It's not in a class with the savage beasts
　And it's tamed with care and patience.

The man that knows what I'm telling you
　Is wiser than many a score;
　　There's few that the heart of a horse can win
　　But a heap that can savage and break them in,
And ram-stam busters that swank around
　With reins and a hackamore.

As I said before, I hit the trail
With that woman by my side,
And all that night without slack or stay
Through the wilderness we took our way,
We left our lives to destiny
And Fate was our only guide.

The Indian's corpse in a patch of grass
I had hid as well as I could,
I dragged him there and crushed him down,
And covered him up from toe to crown,
The time they might lose in finding him
Would make our vantage good.

When they found we were gone I knew for sure
They'd soon be on our track
And I fixed with myself, if the whole tribe came,
And caught us up, they'd find me game,
I'd die like a gaucho, knife in hand,
Before I'd be taken back.

The man who has faced the wilderness
Of its dangers will never joke,
They've died of hunger, many a one,
And left their bones 'neath the blistering sun,
You don't dare even light a fire
For fear of the tell-tale smoke.

It's you and the desert;—flinch or faint
You can bet you won't survive;
Don't hope for help from the empty air,
For God is your only refuge there,
There's a hundred dead to the desert's score,
To one that's come through alive.

A great green plain ringed rim to rim
  With a sky of unbroken blue;
    It's death if once you lose your way
    And here and there you begin to stray,
The man who would cross it should mark this well
  That now I tell to you.

See every day, that your course you lay
  And watch that you hold it dead;
    Don't loiter or waver or roam around,
    Just do your damndest to cover ground;
When you sleep be sure that the way you go
  You're pointing with your head.

Mark well the place on the desert's face
  Where the sun shows its first red rim;
    If there's mist or cloud at the dawning light,
    And you can't get a sight of the sun,—sit tight;
The desert waits for the man that strays
  And it makes short work of him.

God gave their instincts to the beasts
  And wit to every one;
    Man hasn't got less than the beasts I guess
    To find his way in the wilderness,
He's got the winds and the animals
  For guide,—and the stars and sun.

To hide ourselves from the savage bands,
  On the face of the open plain,
    We'd hunt around till some place we found
    To pitch a sheltered camping-ground,
And there we'd lie till the darkness came,
  To take up the trail again.—

We were worn and weary, racked with thirst
  And hungry too, to boot;
    There was many a day no food we saw
    When we got some meat we ate it raw;
And at other times we dug around
  And were glad if we found a root.

But I'll tell no more of the sufferings sore,
  Of our long-drawn tale of woes;
    At last at the end of all our ills,
    We saw far off a range of hills,
And not long after we trod once more
  oThe land where the 'ombú' grows.

With sorrow again for my old friend Cruz
  I felt my bosom swell;
    And in humble thanks to Almighty God
    On my bended knees I kissed the sod
Of that blessed earth that no more is soiled
  By the foot of the infidel.

So God in His mercy guided us
  And back from the wilds we passed;
    He brought us out of the desert grim
    Because of the faith that we put in Him;
To a ranch we came, and they took us in
  And we felt we were safe at last.

To that luckless woman I said goodbye,
  I had brought through the wilderness,
    'I'm off,' I said to her, 'anywhere,
    Let the Government catch me for all I care
For hell against hell, if I've got to choose,
  The frontier's mine, I guess.'—

I'll break off my story here I think,
  And take it up later on;
    My two lost lads I'll present to you,
    Perhaps they've got something to tell us too,
I'd like to hear how life's treated them
  In the years that are lost and gone.

XI

MARTIN FIERRO RELATES HIS MEETING
WITH TWO OF HIS SONS

NOW pass me the crock and I'll take a swig
To cool my warmed-up throat;
And while my youngster tunes his strings
And finds his opening note,
I'll tell you how in my wanderings
I found my two lads once more.
   For many a day I roamed around
And stopped at many a door,
I wanted to know how matters went
In the pickle they call the Government,
But everything I very soon found
Was much as it was before.
So I just lay low and spied the land
And opened my eyes and ears;
It wasn't a bit of good I guessed
To meddle too much with a hornet's nest.
If you've been in trouble you'll understand
The law always holds the winning hand;
And whether it's weeks or months or years
If you're poor they get you in the end.
   But my luck held good—I found one day
A trusty old-time friend,
That put me wise how matters lay,
I was wasting my fears, he said;
For the judge whose nose had been on my trail
These many years was dead.

I had him to thank for ten long years
Of trials and sufferings sore,
And ten's a heap for a man like me
That hasn't got many more.
And this is the way I count my tale
Of trouble and misery;
Three years I lost at the frontier post,
Two years from the law I fled,
And five I spent in our little tent
In the hands of the infidel.
If I'm right, that's ten. And my friend said then,
I could put my mind at ease
That the Government had long forgot
All about my private row,
And none round there ever gave a thought
To the death of that nigger now.

   Though I snuffed his light, it's only right
To say he was part to blame;
I was middling tight—I picked the fight,
And he lost; but all the same
The brute got mad and he forced my hand
For he cut me first I'll swear,
He marked my face,—and you'll understand
That that's no light affair.

   The friend I'm telling of, told me more;
There was no more talk about
The gaucho killer that in a store
I had tumbled insides-out;
There was only one to blame for that
And that one wasn't me;
He dropped in there to look for a brawl
He got what was coming to him—that's all;

He thought I'd be good to practise on
And if I'd been slow, or a simpleton
It would have been him that hit the trail
And me that messed the floor.
   My old friend told me furthermore
That none even told the tale.
Of the ding-dong fight I had the night
I met Cruz, with the police-patrol.
There's nothing in that to worry my soul,
To fight for his life is a man's first right;
They were out for my hide, and they sent a band
By night in the open, arms in hand;
They didn't arrest me in proper form,
But just came on in a yelling swarm,
And shouted out threats to have my life;
Was it any wonder I peeled my knife?
A gaucho outlaw I was, they said,
They were going to get me alive or dead
And it wasn't the Captain that told me that,
Although there was one commanding,
But the first that came up just barked at me,
And whatever I'd done, you'll all agree,
A man's got his rights, and that's no way
To come to an understanding.
   When I got such news I'm bound to say
I was pretty well content,
I felt I could show my face again,
And wherever I liked I went.
Of the little lads that long ago
From their mother and me were riven,
I've found but two; and thanks I owe
For that to the grace of heaven.

Though far and wide round the countryside
I hunted to find their trail,
Though I spared no dint I could get no hint
Of where they might hap to be,

And my hopes at last began to fail
When chance brought them back to me.
For not far off from this very spot
They were holding a racing-meet
And there I went though not a cent
To bless myself with, I'd got;
There were gauchos came from far and near
And many an 'estanciero'
And you'll guess no doubt there were lots about
That had heard of Martin Fierro.
There two of the sons I had thought were lost
Were dressing some mounts by the starting post,
When they heard my name, like a flash they came
And soon were at my side,

They shied a bit as they looked at me,
They had some excuse to stare;
I was tanned like a hide by the desert sun,
And was somewhat the worse for wear;
You can guess we didn't make any show
In front of the crowd. Few words we spoke,
For kisses and hugs are for women folk,
That are built that way; yet all men know
Though a man on his sleeve doesn't wear his heart,
There's a bit of a woman inside of him,
And he often sighs though his face be grim,
And his tears in secret start.
The only thing they've told me yet
Is that my poor wife is dead;
To look for her littlest lamb of all
She went to the town, they said.
And she who was prairie-born and bred
Must have suffered there full sore;
For all she was well set-up and strong,
She was in the hospital ere long,
And in that pen of pains and ills
Lay down to rise no more.
　　There's not a thing in the whole wide earth
That will fill the gap she's left,
When they told me of her I was now bereft
I haven't cried bitterer since my birth;
But it's time to leave sadnesses aside,
Though my life doesn't hold for me much joy
It seems to me that my eldest boy
Is ready to sing us a stave or two;
Let's see how he handles the instrument
And the capers and paces he puts it through.

Though both the lads are strange to you,
Their father here's quite confident;
It's not because they bear my blood
That I think they've got their father's vein,
But because since they teethed they've chewed the cud
Of sorrow and suffering, want and pain;
They've both got spirit and like to play
With fire, more or less in their father's way,
Let them show us their paces, and if they're lame,
On their old crocked sire you can lay the blame.

THE ELDEST SON OF MARTIN FIERRO

XII

THE PRISON

ALTHOUGH by the chip you know the block
  And by its fruit the tree;
    Yet I mind how my mother used to say—
    And I've felt it true before to-day—
That it isn't given the son to speak
  With his father's authority.

You'll remember perhaps how we were left
  With no thatch to shield our heads,
    On the open plain we had to sleep
    Or into some ruined shack we'd creep;
We hadn't a shirt to cover our backs
  Or a poncho for our beds.

Ah, happy is he who has never lived
  Without a sheltering roof;
    It's gospel true what I tell to you,
    Since I was a tot no home I knew,
I had hardly climbed over my cradle's edge
  When I had to beat the hoof.

If anyone helps you, they never spare
  To treat you hard and sore,
    If you're born unlucky it seems to me
    That nothing will better what's got to be;
They chase you off like a wild bull-calf
  If you linger at any door.

Like a homeless beast you wander round,
　For refuge you've got to beg;
　　There's none got use for a waif-and-stray,
　　And orphans are vermin to drive away;
If you've nowhere to go you're like a guitar
　That hasn't a single peg.

I hope my words don't make a cap
　To fit any head that's here;
　　I had no home, I had lost my mother
　　Not a friend was left me, nor a brother
And when the old dog isn't round, there's none
　Of kicking the pup need fear.

One gives him a whack across the back,
　One wallops him over the snout;
　　Another lands him a hail of blows,
　　Till here and there half-dazed he goes,
They'll drive him off if he begs a bone
　With kick and cuff and clout.

And if by chance one takes him in
　He can't call his soul his own;
　　They keep him lean, and his master brags
　　When his rump is showing through his rags,
If he gives him a tattered clout or two
　To cover his skin and bone.

So my boyhood passed, as I'm telling you,
　In hunger and nakedness;
　　I worked like a horse for my meagre keep
　　And in any corner was glad to sleep;
When I grew to a man, alas, for me
　There was waiting a worse distress.

I ask you all to store in mind
    The tale of my sufferings sore;
        In the school of life, where the stripes are fell,
        I've had to learn my lessons well;
    If there's nothing like sorrow to make you think,
        I've thought my share, and more.

If at times with me you don't agree,
    I'll ask you to understand
        That I'm not stuck up in my own conceit;
        And to try to teach I think indiscreet;—
    But to take up my tale, I was working once
        On a ranch as a cattle-hand.

When the law gets a down on a man that's poor
  It's little they heed his pleadings;
    A drover was killed on a near-by ranch,
    I'd been round that way that day by chance,
And I couldn't prove I was innocent
  In the subsequent proceedings.

You can well imagine my hapless plight
  And the depths of my dire despair;
    I had just been finding my feet at last,
    When the law had got me roped and grassed;
And for a killing that wasn't mine,
  I found myself branded there.

As if I wasn't enough, two more
  In the self-same noose they triced;
    The matter got messed up worse and worse
    Till the judge shut his papers with a curse,
'To the town' said he, 'I'll pack you three,
  Trussed up as fast as Christ!

'To the "ornery" justice,' said he, 'you'll go;
  Till then, you're in durance vile.'
    When they tell you that, it's no empty threat.
    For dour and vile is the fare you get;
And 'ornery' was the justice too,—
  As we found in a little while.

It didn't keep us on tenter-hooks,
  Or waste any words, I'll allow.
    The 'ornery' judge laughed at our tale
    And clapped us into the 'ornery' jail
That they call by the high-falutin name
  Of the 'Penitentiary' now.

Although the why of that fick-fack name
  They've never wised me yet;
    In my ignorance it seems to me
    They call it the Penitentiary
By the penitence there with the rest you share,
  When once inside you get.

When the law bucks a gaucho over its ears
  He doesn't fall on a daisy;
    Unless he's got money the law is grim,
    There isn't a man will speak up for him;
The 'gringo' is trickier—if he kills,
  He starts to let on he's crazy.

I've lost the reckoning till this day
  Of the time in that grave I passed;
    If you haven't a friend to jog the judge,
    He'll let you rot before he'll budge,
There ain't no call to try the case
  As long as the prey is fast.

Not a single clue they give to you
  Of what's going to be your fate;
    The days and weeks and months drag on
    Until the last glimmer of hope is gone;
You'd better have left it once for all
  Outside of the prison gate.

They don't care a straw to apply the law,
  Or if a man's innocent;
    The man that invented the prison-cell
    Must have been some soul come back from hell;
There isn't a crime that's big enough
  To fit that punishment.

It's enough to make your heart to break
　No matter how proud you be;
　　The jailers just do as they're told, I know;
　　But they've lived so long in that pen of woe,
That they're dry and hard as the stones and bars
　And that on every side you see.

But it's not by the walls your heart is crushed,
　Nor by fetters your hopes are reft,
　　But the loneliness by night and day
　　And a still so deep one might almost say
That of all the men in the whole wide world
　You're the very last that's left.

No matter how high you hold your comb,
   Or how long your tusks are grown,
     Your hopes will wilt to the very root,
     And your courage shrink like a withered fruit,
When they shut you up in a prison cell
   For month after month alone.

There are no bulls there that toss their horns,
   And snort and paw around,
     They're all tame calves in a little while,
     For to rage at walls is a waste of bile,
The wisest plan is to drop your ears
   And suffer without a sound.

The grief and despair that wait you there
   Inside that stony fence,
     Only they can tell who have borne the chains
     Of Destiny, and its pitiless pains,
So listen to me and you'll profit by
   Another's experience.—

Ah mothers! who watch with tender care
   The steps of the sons you love
     It's the simple truth you'll hear from me;
     The man that is born on the prairie free,
Little dreams what it is within walls to be
   With a roof of stone above.

And daughters and wives and sisters too,
   By whose love some man is blest,—
     Din into their ears that yon prison cell
     Is a torment worse than any hell,
Where no sound is heard but the doleful beat
   Of the heart in one's aching breast.

There never the sun is seen by day,
  By night not a single star;
    No matter how much you growl or whine,
    They'll keep you there till you peak and pine,
And you wet with your tears the floor of stone
  Shut fast behind bolt and bar.

In that still profound you can hear the sound
  Of the blood in your troubled heart;
    And I don't think the souls make a louder din
    In the Pit where the wicked purge their sin;
You may smile at my words, but of what I bore
  They tell but the smallest part.

You keep the count of the weary hours,
  As you count, they drag the more;
    You lean your brow on the cold stone wall
    And count your tears as they form and fall,
And you count by your pulse the time they take
  To dry on the stony floor.

The terrible silence beats you down
  Till it stifles your very breath;
    It tames the proudest heart ere long,
    And makes short work of the brave and strong,
In that stillness there, you could hear, I swear,
  The very steps of Death.

Your thoughts run round inside your mind
  Till your very head gets sore;
    Then after your thoughts you start to run
    And catch them and look at them one by one,
And I'll tell you men, that you catch some then
  That you never saw well before.

I thought of my brothers and mother dear,
   That so long had been lost to me;
      Every memory that I kept in store,
      In those weary days I turned o'er and o'er
And many a scene I called to mind
   That perhaps never more I'd see.

There's none like the son of the pampas wide,
   Will worse a prison thole,
      When he's shut inside of a prison gate
      The way he suffers is desperate,
It seems to me that's a misery
   That can cow the stoutest soul.

I fretted there in my narrow cell
   And as day by day crept o'er me,
      I'd pace the floor from wall to door
      And there to myself say o'er and o'er:
'What wouldn't I give to be on a horse,
   With the boundless plain before me!'

Your heart grows faint, as in ceaseless plaint,
   Your days and nights you spend;
      And to punish you, if too loud you bark,
      They shut you up in the pitchy dark;
Ah! jail is a tether that doesn't break
   And a bar that doesn't bend!

Every dismal thought in the whole wide world,
   Comes there to visit you;
      By your side they sit down hard and fast,
      Till you've got to bow your head at last;
Misfortune's got lots of kith and kin,
   And a bunch of cronies too.

You'll weep in vain—it won't help your pain,
 Nor comfort your misery;
  Your tears may drip till your eyes run dry,
  Not a moment's peace all your tears will buy,
While you see the joys of your vanished days,
 With the eyes of your memory.

No gleam of hope ever lights the gloom
 Inside those merciless walls;
  A man that's as tough as an axle-pin,
  When once to that hell they've stuffed him in,
Though he rage and rail, soon droops his tail,
 And to sullen silence falls.—

It seems at first one's heart would burst,
 From fury and sheer despair;
  But it's not a bit of good to shout,
  There's nothing to do but stick it out.
He's a lucky man that in such a place,
 Can call to his mind a prayer!

If you know a prayer send it up to God,
 He's the only one will hear you;
  The world goes on, but you're left to rot,
  And even your very name's forgot;
And suffering's always worse to bear
 When there isn't a kind heart near you.

From my pain and grief I had no relief;
 I began to wilt indeed;
  Before many months had passed away
  My face was lined and my hair was grey
And often then I regretted sore,
 I had never learnt to read.—

When your fury's spent, discouragement
　　Creeps over you like a blight;
　　　　It lay on my life like an evil curse
　　　　And every day it got worse and worse,
On the stony pave of that living grave,
　　My tears fell day and night.

There were some had friends that now and then
　　Would lighten their misery,
　　　　But while I was there, I tell you true,
　　　　I never set eyes on a face I knew;
For who had I, who would bear the cost
　　Of coming to comfort me?

For a cheery smile or a kindly word,
　　Of the men that kept that hell,
　　　　A blessing on them from God we'd ask;
　　　　But we never found that a tiring task,
For pity's no part of a jailer's job,—
　　If he feels it, he hides it well.

I can't tell half what I suffered there
　　In that cell with its iron grille;
　　　　My sight got so used to locks and bars,
　　　　It seemed on my eyes they had left their scars,
And when I shut them, in my sleep
　　I kept on seeing them still.

．　　．　　．　　．　　．　　．

ₒNot a drink of 'maté' they let you have,
   They punished you if you spoke;
      It's against the rules for a man to sing,
      To lighten the load of his suffering,
And worst of all it seems to me,
   They won't even let you smoke.

When you tighten up Justice overmuch
   It's plumb unjust I guess;
      The wretch that gets into the law's grim clutch
      Gets no law at all when he gets too much;
A noose or a knife is more merciful
   Than that terrible loneliness.

We'd talk to the walls; we'd talk to the bars,
   Since we couldn't talk to men;
      But they soon came round and made us quit,
      Though our teeth we grit on that bitter bit,
For it ain't no good to lash your heels,
   When you're fast in the branding pen.

And muzzled there in our dumb despair,
   Round our dismal cells we'd plod;
      When a man can't speak to a fellow man,
      He's nearer to brute than to human clan;
For the power of speech is the best of all
   The gifts of Almighty God.

It doesn't fit in my simple wit,
   What good those guards can find,
      When a man is shut in a prison cell,
      In treating him like a beast as well,
And stopping him using the two best gifts
   Heaven gave to our human kind.

For of all the blessings, it seems to me,—
  (Though I haven't a learnéd mind)
    That God spilled out on our mortal race,
    There are two that have first and second place;
Though speech is first at the winning post
  Yet friendship's close behind.

Whoever you are and whatever you've done,
  I figure the law's too hard,
    That shuts you from all the world away,
    And keeps you in torment night and day,
From the sight and sound of your fellow men,
  And the gifts of God debarred.

The silence shrivels up your heart,
  The solitude's like a ghost.
    You live in fear of you don't know what;
    And to torture a man when he's safely caught,
Is just as bad as to savage a colt,
  When it's tied to a snubbing-post.

You begin to doubt that you won't get out
  Till it's you for the burial-yard.
    There's nothing worse when you're in distress,
    Than to have to go through it in loneliness;
No matter how deep you're in the dumps,
  You'll get out—if you've got a pard.

There's some are wiser than me perhaps—
  I'm putting this forward, only—
    When they nailed up Christ on that awful tree
    They weren't all bad; and it seems to me,
They gave Him two others that came to hand
  Just to keep Him from feeling lonely.

I haven't got books, for I never went
　To a reading and writing master;
　　But I'm sure no book says it's any good
　　To make a man better with solitude;
To have someone to talk to when you're sick
　Is better than any plaster.

　　　·　　·　　·　　·　　·　　·

Remember well my hapless tale—
　Not a tittle I've falsified—
　　But I'll give his due to the Governor:
　　There's some little things I've to thank him for,
Though he's got to look tough, and be grim and gruff,
　I think he's a saint inside.

And the jailers too have their jobs to do,
　And I guess they do what they can;
　　But all they do doesn't change the fact
　　That every prisoner there is racked
With a long-drawn ache that's enough to break
　The heart of any man.

Pack safe away in your memory
　All this I've been telling you;
　　If you think I've only been making a song
　　To pass the time—well, you'll all be wrong;
And perhaps some day that's not far away
　You'll find for yourselves it's true.

Attend to me, or perhaps your tears
　Will drip on some prison floor;
　　Just keep to the straight and narrow way
　　Or you're sure to rue it on reckoning day;
I haven't run out of arguments,—
　I could give you a hundred more.

But I'll wind up my song, for it's overlong,
And I'll bid you all farewell.
I only hope that you'll bear in mind
The tale of the woes that I've left behind.
What else can he tell who has spent his days
Shut fast in a prison cell?

THE SECOND SON OF MARTIN FIERRO

XIII

MARTIN FIERRO'S SECOND SON BEGINS TO
TELL HIS STORY

L ET no one doubt what I'm going to sing
    Though at times he may feel inclined,—
      It's a bit of a mouthful—that I'll say,
      But I'll tackle it in the Fierro way,
My heart is glib, though my tongue may jib,
    And sometimes lag behind.

For ten long years 'mid woes and fears
    And trials and troubles sore,
      We roamed the plains, with the grass for bed,
      And never a roof but the sky o'erhead,
And many a day we were turned away
    When we stopped at a stranger's door.

There's none to care for the wanderer,
    He gets nothing but kicks and scraps;
      When our father went, we orphan chicks
      oWere just like a bunch of mavericks,
And off we rolled like so many beads
    When the string of the rosary snaps.

Like the rest of us, I wandered off,
    I had only the rig I packed;
      Till an aunt of mine, who was old and frail,
      Got news of me, and I left the trail;
She gave me a bed and a roof to my head,
    And never a thing I lacked.

The dear old soul simply pampered me,
  My days went by like a song;
    Like a silly boy I must confess
    I lived in a round of idleness;
But alas full soon, I found no boon
  Is apt to last for long.

She doted on me, and I tell you this,
  It wasn't a passing fad;
    For years she had lived by herself alone,
    She hadn't a son of her very own,
So she mothered me; and when she died,
  She left me all she had.

We laid her out; but she wasn't stiff,
  When the Judge was on the spot;
    'You must know,' said he, 'that the law takes charge
    Of the whole round-up—it's middling large—
And the house and land, and two flock of sheep,—
  I think that makes the lot.'

He had lots of law, and the gift of gab,
  I've never met lawyer cuter;
    He said to me: 'Though the whole outfit
    ○Has been left you, you're a minor yet,
You can't own anything—you're too young—
  So I'll have to appoint a tutor.'

He made up a list of everything,
  For a learnéd man was he—
    When he saw all the dough was in the cake,
    And nothing to do but to leave it to bake,
He named a boss for the whole bang lot
  And off he hurried me.

I soon began to get ragged then,
  My poncho was holed and torn,
    oMy 'chiripá' wouldn't stop the wind
    And though I've never been tender-skinned,
The heat and the cold fair made me dance
  Like a sheep that's newly shorn.

Full desperate was my wretched state,
  My hopes grew less and less;
    Like a wandering beggar I had to live,
    Not a sign of life did the Justice give;
I often thought what my aunt would say
  Could she see my nakedness.

I lost my count of the time I passed
  In rags and misery;
    Like an ownerless horse that all may ride
    I wandered about from side to side,
Till at last to the tutor I was sent
  Who was going to take charge of me.

XIV

OLD 'VIZCACHA'

A TOUGH old geezer took me off—
　　I sized him with half an eye—
　　　He had a face like the criminal code,
　　　As sly an old thief as ever rode;
o'Vizcacha' was the elegant name
　　They knew the old rascal by.

I can guess what the Justice had in mind—
　　For all his cunning ways—
　　　But it's not my way to nurse a grudge,
　　　So I'll leave his secret to the Judge.—
A real old-timer my tutor was
　　As you'll scarce find nowadays.

A veteran up to every trick,
　　And grim as a bull he was;
　　　oHe went around on a 'moro' horse
　　　And trouble to him was a matter of course;
From wearing his stirrups between his toes
　　oHis feet were like parrots' claws.

Some mongrel hounds hung always round
　　The trail of that ancient sinner;
　　　To curse at them was his sole delight,
　　　There were six at least; and every night
He butchered somebody else's cow
　　To give those curs their dinner.

There wasn't a brand that night by night,
  Some prime head didn't lose;
    He left the beef to his snarling pack,
    And toted the hide on his horse's back,
○In the 'pulpería' he bartered it
  ○For 'yerba,' smokes, and booze.

As a flinty-fisted bargainer
  In my life I've met his mate.
    The barefaced thief, for that stolen skin,
    Would squeeze the last drop of watered gin,
And he and the bar-keep there and then
  ○Made out the certificate.

At shearing-time his meddlesome tricks
　　Were the bane of the overseers;
　　　　If anyone happened to nick a sheep
　　　　The sour old codger would thraw and threep;
But that never stopped him making off
　　With a fleece and a pair of shears.

He gave me a terrible leathering once,
　　Until for help I cried;
　　　　In the shack of some basques I kicked a pup;
　　　　In a rage he took the matter up;
But he lifted some green hides off the fence,
　　As soon as we got outside.

Aijuna! I thought—you'll pay for that,
　　I'll put a pole in your spokes,
　　　　When I see my chance you'll catch it hot;
　　　　I'll make you lose that habit you've got
oOf cropping the hair from the tails of mares
　　That belong to other folks.

He flew in a rage another time,
　　And I barely got off scot-free;
　　　　I killed a vizcacha, and when I got back
　　　　And told him, he roared like a maniac,
As he grabbed his whip: 'Don't ever dare
　　To name that beast to me!'

I had to dodge him a day or two,
　　He was feeling so mighty sore;
　　　　I saw if I didn't humour his whims,
　　　　The old ruffian might break my head or limbs;
I figured he had some grudge at the beasts,
　　And I never named them more.

oWe cut out a bunch of broom-tails once
  On a ranch one afternoon;
    They were mostly lame—he downed a few
    And was stripping their tails without more ado,
When I saw the owner coming along
  And I guessed there'd be trouble soon.

I didn't let on, and the man came up,
  He looked real riled, I'll say,
    He jumped off his horse—not a word he said—
    He whirled his stock-whip round his head
And he landed a crack on my tutor's back
  You could hear half a mile away.

Don Vizcacha came clear up in the air
  As if he was made of springs;
    He didn't know what had hit him, or where,
    And which way he streaked he didn't care,
He managed to get on his horse and bolt,
  Without gathering up his things.

You'll think perhaps the old thief was cured
  Of his tricks when he'd had that fright;
    No sirs; he carried on just the same,
    But he changed the way he worked his game,
He hobbled the mares that he caught by day,
  And came back for their tails at night.

That's the kind of man, for my guardian
  The Judge had been pleased to name;
    He had always been a ne'er-do-weel;
    There wasn't a time when he didn't steal,
And far and wide round the countryside
  He had nothing but evil fame.

When the Judge put him in charge of me
　　Until I had time to grow,
　　　He said I'd find him a proper man,
　　　Who'd care for me as a father can,
He'd teach me to work, and bring me up
　　In the way that a boy should go.

But I ask you, what was I like to learn
　　But a lot of sinful lore,
　　　From a land-louping scapegrace, hung with rags,
　　　That lived like a leech in the fens and quags,
A gully-raking veteran scamp,
　　Bad-biled as a mangy boar?

Not a thing was known he could call his own
　　But the tatters he used to wear,
　　　A splay-wheeled cart, a filthy pack,
　　　And the ramshackle walls of a roofless shack,
That for more years than men called to mind,
　　Had served him for a lair.

When an end he'd made of his nightly raid
　　He'd go off to that den to hide;
　　　I often hankered to know just what
　　　The hoary old thief in that hut had got,
But I couldn't find out, for never once
　　He let me get inside.

I'd some saddle-cloths that once were wool,
　　But now all their nap had lost;
　　　Though mother-naked I almost was,
　　　The callous old brute didn't care two straws;
Outside of his shelter he made me sleep
　　Though the ground was white with frost.

In his callow youth he married a wife,—
　　I doubt it—but so they told;
　　　And I heard this more from a man I knew,—
　　　Which I haven't a doubt was gospel-true,—
That he laid her dead with a crack on the head
　　For serving his 'maté' cold.

When he'd murdered her, as a widower
　　For himself he had to fend;
　　　For a woman to be that wretch's wife,
　　　Would have meant every minute to risk her life,
In one of his fits, some day for sure,
　　She'd have come to the same bad end.

I knew the nights when he dreamt of her—
　　For he'd wake with a dreadful yell;
　　　When at last he fell sick and took to bed
　　　One day that damned old sinner said
That he heard her shouting in his dreams
　　She was waiting for him in hell.

XV

THE COUNSELS OF OLD VIZCACHA

HE was so soured up that he hardly spoke
If it wasn't to disagree;
To amuse himself he would scratch around
  ○Drawing brands with his finger on the ground,
And when he got drunk his habit was
To give some advice to me.

In his shoddy poncho I see him yet
Sitting cross-legged on the ground;
He would take a swig at the crock of gin,
And something after this style begin:
'Don't trouble to halt at any place
  ○Where you see lean dogs around.

'Man's first look-out is to see he keeps
　　His hide from getting holed;
　　　　Remember this that I say, my lad,
　　　　It's the best advice you've ever had—
oThe devil is sly, for he's built that way,
　　But he's slyer because he's old.

o'Whatever you do, keep in with the judge,
　　What he says, store well in mind;
　　　　If he starts to get angry, drop your head,
　　　　Don't get in his way while he's seeing red;
A paling to rub your ribs against
　　Is a comfort, you'll often find.

'He's the boss of the team; and when he talks
　　If you're wise keep your mouth well shut;
　　　　The harnessed bullock should not provoke
　　　　The driver that sits on the wagon yoke,
oHe gets the leaders, with the spike
　　And the wheelers with the butt.

'The man that wears the jauntiest airs
　　And swaggers all round about,
　　　　Soon changes his looks when he hits bad luck,
　　　　You can't tell him then from the common ruck;
The wildest colts come in to drink
　　At the well when they feel the drought.

'Just look at the rat—it's sleek and fat
　　Though it dens in dirt and grime;
　　　　You copy it—don't change your lair,
　　　　Stay put where your nose first sniffed the air;
The cow that's changed from her grazing ground
　　oGets late in the calving-time.

'Remember, Fierro,' he'd say again
   Between swig and swig of gin:
     'Whatever you do don't put belief
     In any man or you'll come to grief;
By a woman that weeps or a hound that limps
   Don't ever be taken in.

'If the world comes down about your ears,
   Don't let it your sleep endanger;
     Man's finest gift it seems to me
     Is to have the donkey's memory,
Though some complain that it's got no brain,
   It never forgets its manger.

'Let him heat up the oven and blow the fire
   That's the owner of the batter;
     As for me, by the fire I just mooch around
     Till the crust of the loaf is nice and browned,
The pig may be greedy that eats its young
   But what does it care?—it's fatter!

'The old scarred fox is the hardest one
   To take with trap or ruse;
     Don't grudge the effort or spare the pains,
     When there's none but yourself to share the gains;
The cow that gives the richest milk
   Is the one that longest chews.

'When you've got your dinner, take my tip;
   Don't spread the news around;
     Till you've got it down don't laugh and joke
     And get on the sky-line of other folk,
 ○The runaway never gets off clear
   If it heads for the rising ground.

'I keep to my beat and I'm never short
   Of a joint and a souse of gin,
      Just stick like a leech to this simple rule
      And you'll sleep every night with your bellyfull;
The ant is wise for it wastes no time
   Exploring an empty bin.

'It's not a bit use getting envious
   Of somebody else's luck;
      If you see another that's struck it rich
      Don't start butting in and spoil his pitch;
For each little pig at his private tit
   Is the proper way to suck.

'The world's a sow where the strongest suck
   And the poor get the mean go-by;
      There's some like the kid that daintily nip
      The nipple's point between lip and lip,
While the calf gets a grip and gets its fill
   Before you can wink your eye.

'If you don't want trouble don't get spliced
   Or of troubles you'll hit a heap;
      But if on some filly you drop your noose
      Look well at the bunch before you choose,
For a thing that others are wanting too
   Is a thing that's hard to keep.

'And woman's an animal, my boy,
   I don't get any road,
      She'll fall for the man that's quick and game,
      But keep your eye on her all the same
For her heart's as roomy and big and soft
   As the belly of any toad.'

And he'd ramble on: 'You're a foal, my son,
  Your eye-teeth barely sprout;
    Remember—an old bull's telling you—
    Wherever you go and whatever you do,
Never let any man come up too near
  ○On the side that your knife comes out.

'At times in life you'll need your knife,
  That's all you know for true,
    But you don't know when; so day and night
    Keep it ready to hand, and keen and bright,
○But don't drag at the hilt, unless you've got
  Some work for the blade to do.

'You can work like a slave, but unless you save
  Some day you'll beg your clothes,
    If you haven't got thrift in your bone and blood
  Some day with your muzzle you'll plough the mud.
○"Pot-belly born, puts belts to scorn,"
  The good old saying goes.

'Blow here, blow there, it's little I care,—
  Come rain on my weathered pelt;—
    If I hit bad luck I tip my chin
    And take a good swig at my crock of gin;
If I'm wet outside I even up
  With a sousing inside my belt.

'Little cockerel—remember well
  My advice—you'll hear lots worse—
    The lessons I give you don't forget;
    I'm an old game-cock, and a winner yet,
You won't find me crowing round the ring
  Without my fighting spurs.'

With such-like saws without a pause
  He'd fill up an hour or more,
    He'd keep me sitting beside his knee,
    While he went on educating me;
Till flat on his back, 'mid his mongrel pack,
  Dead drunk he'd start to snore.

XVI

THE DEATH OF OLD VIZCACHA

AT last the old fellow took to bed
And I saw him get worse and worse;
   When I thought for sure he was going to kick
  oI fetched a 'culandrera' quick;
I asked her to do what she could for him
And I said I'd be his nurse.

As soon as she saw him she said to me,
  'My science has come too late;
   In the loop of Death he's hard and fast,
   When he feels the jerk he'll soon be grassed;
oThere's a tabernacle as big as your fist
  Just under his omoplate.'

The proverb says that in every herd
  There's always a goring bull:
   One butted in then, from near the door.
   'I hope,' said he, 'you won't take this sore:
A "tabernacle's" not the word—
  What he had was a tubercule.'

The singer came back: 'Thanks, smarty-Jack,
   For pointing out the error;
     I don't think this is the time or place
     For outsiders to talk, but in any case
It was "tabernacle" was the word
   That was used by the "culandrera." '

The man at the door wasn't done for yet,
   He got his own back quick:—
     'Here goes for another bolas-shot,
     I'll see your hand, and take bank and pot;
A "curandera's" the proper name
   For a woman that heals the sick.'

'Too many cooks' the singer said,
   'Are sure to spoil the soup;
     I'll ask that cheap skate by the door
     To stop butting in; and I'll add this more:
I didn't know this was the meeting place
   Of a literary group.'

But I'll take up the tale of my tutor again
   Before someone gets up his dander,
     And I'll ask the professor over there,
     With my lack of learning to try to bear;
For no one ever yet span a yarn
   Wasn't bettered by some bystander.

He was pretty near dead, as I have said
   And day by day got worse;
     He was nearing his end, it was plain to see;
     He fair put the fear of death in me;
He had a mouth like one of the damned
   That did nothing but rave and curse.

Long wintry nights in the roofless shack
On his heap of rags he'd yell;
To vary his ravings and complaints
He would curse at God, and damn the Saints,
And howl on the devil to come for him
And carry him off to hell.

A man must be pretty black inside
To die like a fear-mad beast;
If his eye on some holy relic lit,
He would shiver and shake in a foaming fit,
Like a man with an evil spirit does
When he's sprinkled by the priest.

My life wasn't safe inside his reach,
For the man was clean insane;
I didn't want him to crawl about,
So whatever he couldn't do without,
I reached to him from across the shack
On the end of a good long cane.

I was often minded to leave him there—
The truth I must confess—
To leave him alone to spill his gall,
To rage and rave and blaspheme and bawl,
Till Death came along and put an end
To that bundle of wickedness.

The time came along when he couldn't speak—
A bell to his wrist I tied;—
In a storm of rags he kicked and thrashed,
And clawed at the walls and foamed and
gnashed,
Till at last in a heap mid his snarling dogs
He stretched out his neck and died.

XVII

THE INVENTORY OF VIZCACHA'S GOODS

THE sight of the old fellow lying dead
   Fairly bristled up my hairs;
     I called the 'alcalde' of the place,
   And soon he came round with an ill enough grace;
He brought three or four neighbours along with him
   To wind up the deceased's affairs.

'God rest his soul' said one veteran,
   That had seen better days,
     'I hope his sins are forgiven by now,
     In his times he was slick,—that I'll allow;
And a tidy bunch of stolen calves
   He used to put to graze.'

'That's how he began,' the alcalde said,
   'Of the dead I don't speak ill;
     I never knew one got in more rows
     For butchering other people's cows;
In the end we had to prohibit him
   From making a single kill.

'In his younger days he could fork a colt
   With the best round this bit of land;
     He'd shut himself up in the horse-corral,
     And pick out the liveliest animal,
And without any help he'd back the beast,
   And gallop it to a stand.

'He was always at odds with everyone,
    Because of a way he had;
        He'd mix up his sheep with other flocks;
        When they sorted them out the sly old fox
Got more than his share—then he'd come to me,
    And swear he'd been done down bad.'

'God take him to glory,' chimed in a third,
    'A bigger thief never died.
        As a stealer of sheep he earned his fame,
        And a master he was at his special game;
ₒHe'd bury the head without leaving a trace,
    And then he would sell the hide.

'He had a habit of dropping in
    To hobnob with the men
        Around the fire, and once he got
        His hands on the circling maté-pot,—
"I cut and I keep the bank," he'd say,
    And it didn't come round again.

'When he skewered an asado he was worse;
    The old guzzler! I see him yet,
        So that nobody else should ask a bit,
        He'd first lay a dreadful curse on it,
Then to make assurance doubly sure
    On the sizzling meat he'd spit.

'Of that filthy trick of his, one night,
    He was cured for all his life;
        A mulatto deserter, a friend of his,
        That helped him in all his rogueries,
oWas with him—"Barullo" his nick-name was,
    A devil, and quick with his knife.

'When the old fellow there on a juicy roast
    Performed his accustomed rite;
        "Barullo" who was getting all set to dine,
        Jumped up and roared "You dirty swine,
I'll teach you to swallow your slobber down
    And not spoil my appetite."

'And on the word he jumped at him,—
    As he jumped his knife came out,—
        La Pucha! the nigger was quick at the draw
        A niftier knifer I never saw;
Someone struck up his arm; or the old man there
    Would soon have been kicking about.

‘ "Barullo" was out for Vizcacha's blood,
 But the wise old man was wary;
  When he saw the nigger was wild to the hair,
  Not even his dinner could keep him there;
He streaked for the door and leapt for his horse
 And high-tailed for the open prairie.

‘Of that cursed custom anyway
 He was broken that night for good;
  He didn't dare come back to the place;
  For a week he scarcely showed his face,
He hung around in the swamps and brakes
 And fended as best he could.’

They went on with their gossip-mongering there—
　　There's heaps that I haven't told—
　　　　I was sitting quiet by the old man's bed;
　　　　Though he'd been a scamp,—to myself I said:
'Good God! what a rosary and a half
　　For a corpse that's barely cold!'

The alcalde then began to list
　　The goods of the late deceased;
　　　　From holes and corners he fished out scraps
　　　　Of rags and bones and rattle-traps,
A rumblegairy magpie's nest,
　　Half a hundred years old at least.

He tumbled out lassos and halter-ropes,
　　And thongs, and tag-ends of pelts,
　　　　Yoke-leathers, hobbles, a sheaf of whips,
　　　　And reins and pack-ropes and raw-hide strips,
Head-stalls and bridles and bits galore,
　　And piles of old leather belts.

There were nose-bands and head-straps and hackamores,
　　And a hundred other things,
　　　　Stirrups and bolas and saddles and spurs,
　　　　Kettles and pots and old canisters,
And buckles and girths and a great big bunch
　　Of cut-off cincha-rings.

He turned up some battered cattle-bells,
　　Awls, knives, and hanks of hair,
　　　　Some saddle-covers and mouldy bags,
　　　　And one or two blankets worn to rags,
And a score or so of old broken boots,
　　Without two that would make a pair.

There was any amount of sardine tins,
  He had filched from the country store;
    Some ponchos riddled with rent and hole—
    'Hold on!' the alcalde said: 'Bless my soul!'
As out of the lot popped an old ink-pot
  He had lost two years before!

He said very stern, as he pursed his lips:
  'Well, he's gone to his reckoning.
    The sly old ant! What a store he's piled!
    Whatever I say of him's far too mild;
I'll inform the Judge; I won't have him say
  We stand for this kind of thing.'

I was thunder-struck amid all that ruck
  And hiddley-pig caboodle;
    Some were nosing among the jumbled wares,
    And saying that this or that was theirs,
But it seemed to me that kind of talk
  Was just so much flapdoodle.

They poked and smelt, and peered and felt,
  Every nook of that filthy hovel,
    Not a single crack they didn't ransack;
    Then said the alcalde: 'Let's get back,—
We'll put him to grass with his teeth turned up,—
  I'll send out a man with a shovel.'

Though it hadn't been any father of mine
  Had owned that squirrel's hoard;
    The alcalde turned as he left the shack,
    And patted me kindly on the back;
'You're heir to the lot my lad,' said he,
  'And we'll see it all packed and stored.

'And everything will be arranged
  In the most approved of ways.
    From these neighbours I'll choose some kind señor,
    To be our late friend's executor;
Things aren't done dirty or underhand,
  As they were in the bad old days.'

'My God,' thought I; 'I'm so starving poor,
  That whenever I move I rattle;
    And they're making me heir to all this gear—
    Well, all I can say is, it's mighty queer.
I'd like the Judge to tell me first
  What's become of my old aunt's cattle!'

XVIII

THE BURIAL

SO off they went, for the funeral
    To arrange, as I have said;
      I shudder to think of that dreadful night,
      At times I nearly howled with fright;
I was all alone in that desolate shack,
    In the dark, with the dogs and the dead.

    ◦I took off my scapulary there,
      To lay on the sinner's breast;
        To Almighty God on my bended knee,
        For the soul of my tutor I made my plea,
To see fit in his mercy infinite
    In heaven to give him rest.

Not a rite I spared, for all I was scared
    As anyone well might be;
      Like a son,—though I shook in every limb,—
      I stuttered a rosary over him
While I kissed the blesséd scapular
    That my mother had given to me.

'Dear mother of mine,' at times I called,
    'What fate has been yours, God knows,—
      The tears I shed you would shed for me
      Could you see your son in his misery,
Alone this night in this fearful plight
    Bowed down by a thousand woes.'

As I cried in the dark I heard the hounds
  Around me sniff and prowl;
    My hair stood straight up on my head
    And to put the last touch on my growing dread
Those dogs in chorus all at once
  Set up an unearthly howl.

May God forbid that any man here
  The like should ever bear,
    The eerie dark, the roofless shack
    The sprawling corpse and the howling pack,
Nearly cracked my wits into little bits
  And started me drivelling there.

The old wives round about those parts
  Used to say, as old wives do;
    When a dog by night begins to wail
    The Devil, complete with hoofs and tail,
Is seen for sure—in my ignorance
  I took it for gospel-true.

So there in a jiffy I left the rats
  To make free of that dreadful midden;
    I guessed there was no one could keep me back;
    Of my rags and tags I made a pack,
And I took to my heels without choosing my trail
  Or waiting till I was bidden.

    .   .   .   .   .   .

They told me that that same afternoon
  ₒA peon with a spade came round,
    He dug a hole and tumbled him in,—
    They didn't wake him or shrive his sin—
And the next day at morning one of his hands
  Was sticking out of the ground.

The man that told the thing to me
  Was the gaucho that buried him;
    (The memory makes me shiver yet
    And I turn in my sleep if I dream of it.)
He told me the old man's famished dogs
  Had gnawed the flesh off the limb.

Perhaps some part of the blame was mine
  For having left him there;
    When I came back they told me too,
    And this I know for a fact is true:
That for miles around not a soul was found
  Would go near that ruined lair.

In the roofless hut the vermin swarmed
  O'er the pile of abandoned loot;—
    It shuddered the flesh to the very bone
    If you happened to pass the place alone;—
And all night long, on the roof-tree fork,
  A giant owl would hoot.

It took me some time to collect my wits,
  I wandered from side to side;
    My clothes were nothing but tatters and tags,
    I'd have robbed a scarecrow of its rags;
I dreamt every night of old men and dogs,
  And scraps of rotten hide.

XIX

REMEDIES FOR AN UNREQUITED LOVE

○ LIKE a masterless man I roamed around,
  I was poor but trouble-free;
   On the Judge I kept a wary eye—
   When you're bit by a dog you get kennel-shy;
 I knew if he caught me, on the spot
  A new tutor he'd name for me.

'I'll take good care,' he had told me once,
  'Of all your heritage;
   If you shut it up under lock and key,
   Not as safe it would be—just leave it to me,
○The titles I'll hold till you're thirty years old,
  Which is when you're of legal age.'

So I had to wait till the lawful date
  Of my coming-of-age to fall;
   I had only my rig-out to call my own,
   I suited my ways to myself alone,
As much good on the whole, as an odd pair of 'bolas'
  That's short of the handling-ball.

The years passed on, I grew to a man,
  I learnt my lessons well—
   In the school of life, be it soon or late
   Man's taught to be wise by the knocks of Fate,
Till at length to an unrequited love
  A wretched prey I fell.

Of all the tales of my ups and downs
   I've come to the knottiest part;
      I got sick with love like the cattle-blain;
      Not a friend I had to salve my pain,
A widow it was that flouted me,
   And trampled my pining heart.

It's the way of man since the world began
   To say it's a burning shame
      If others don't jump with his plan or whim;
      They're wrong; or Fate's got a down on him,
While perhaps all the time, if the truth were told
   He's got only himself to blame.

I was sick and sore, and the more I bore,
   The worse seemed to grow my smarts;
      I prayed to heaven in my misery
      To send for my torment some remedy,
oWhen a fortune-teller they told me of,
   With a cure for lovesick hearts.

I didn't take on at the first go off,
   Some trap in the grass I smelt,
      But once when a sleepless night I'd passed,
      I went to pay him a call at last,
And to see if he'd cure me, I emptied out
   Every cent I had in my belt.

For all I was offhand with my tale
   And tried to act light and chatty;
      My tongue got in knots and my face went red,
      And I swallowed a lump when the hermit said:
'My brother; they've cast the blight on you
   By something they put in your "maté."

'They've tried to bewitch you, and but for me
  Of your life they'd have made short shrift;'
    Then he got out an ostrich-feather there,
    And he stroked me down with a solemn air,
  And he said: 'I received from the Sacred Cross
  This wonderful healing gift.'

'You must curse,' said he, 'as I'll tell you how,
  Every soul that you ever knew,
    Like that you'll get your enemy sure,
    There's nothing like cursing to start the cure;
  And you mustn't keep to the living ones,
  You must curse the dead ones too.'

He said on some scrap of the widow's clothes
  I must kneel and say my prayers,
    It must be in front of a plant of rue,
    I wasn't to think any other would do;
  'That'll cure this passion, provided,' he said,
  'The widow is unawares.'

From the widow I filched a scrap of cloth,
  For some rue I hunted round;
    I knelt and prayed for an hour or more,
    Till my neck was stiff and my knees were sore,
  But I might as well have spared my pains
  For all the relief I found.——

To eat dwarf-thistles another time
  That sage prescribed for me;
    I don't pretend that I understood
    How thistles were going to do me good,
  But I bloodied my jowl in a thistle-patch
  By trying that remedy.

At length with so much doctoring,
  It seemed to me now and then,
    That I got some relief from my wretchedness,
    And the pains in my heart grew less and less,
  But whenever the widow crossed my path
  I soon got worse again.

Again on the trail to the hermit's hut
  I went with my suffering,
    Very graciously he took his fee,
    And then that old rascal said to me:
'You must hang like a rosary round your neck
  Three crickets on a string.'

The last time I consulted him
  And paid him—more's the grief—
    He said to me: 'No, I will not admit
    That my science has lost its virtue yet,
I'll take you out of this woman's toils,—
  This time you'll get sure relief.

'Keep up your heart; for this wondrous art
   I know from A to Z,
      Though it's greek of course to the likes of you;
      Without anyone knowing what you do,
In a pot of milk boil up three curls,
   That you've snipped from a black man's head.'

I had got to the point where I had my doubts
   Of my doctor's scholarship;
      I said to myself: 'This rascal here,
      Won't make a success of me—that's clear—
It's better to let a hen take its chance,
   Than kill it to cure the pip.'

So all forlorn I went lingering on,
   With my sorrows as best I could;
      Till the priest called me up—for the good of my soul
      He served me a long-nebbed rigmarole;
And he told there, to the church's care,
   The widow was vowed for good.

And he added these words which I've never forgot:
   'Mark well what I'm telling you;
      When this woman's husband, now deceased,
      Was about to die, he called a priest,
      And he said that no man was to have her to wife
      For all the term of her natural life;
And before he departed this earthly lot
   That oath she swore him true.

'And that vow she took she must carry out,
   Or against the Church rebel;
      So now you know; and from this day on,
      Just leave the woman in peace my son,
If she breaks her oath (I warn you both)
   You'll be sorry, too late, in hell.'

I didn't need more to open my eyes;
  My passion began to cool;
    ₒI saw the knave coming out of the pack
    And to hang round the widow I didn't go back;
I was better cured than with thistles or rue
  Or crickets or nigger's wool.

And a friend soon after gave me the tip
  That the Judge had been told by the priest,
    That I was a vagabond cumber-ground,
    A harum-scarum that loafed around,
That he'd like to see me driven away,
  From his district at the least.

I haven't a doubt that that was why
  The Judge picked up my track;
    Not a thing he charged I had said or done,
    But he roped me in before I could run,
And with the draft he had rounded up,
  For the frontier I had to pack.

Of all I owned I've told you now,
  How misfortune quick bereft me;
    Of hanging round widows I'm cured, I'll say,
    But I think I'll call on that Judge some day,
And ask him what's become of the farm
  And the cows that my old aunt left me.

XX

INTRODUCING A NEW ARRIVAL

SO merrily mid the company
    That had gathered around them there,
    Our friend Martin and his long-lost sons
Kept up their festivity;
Ten weary years as I have told
Between their parted ways had rolled;
At finding each other 'twas plain to see
They weren't shy to hide their glee.
Then out of the bunch around the door
A stranger stepped to the open floor,
He said in that jolly gathering there
He'd be mighty glad if they'd let him share.
A youngster he was, with a pleasant face;
He carried himself with a jaunty air,
And was well set-up as any there,

He hadn't been long around that place.
The neighbours said that for many a year
He'd served in a post on the far frontier;
At the last race-meet some had heard it said,
He had fleeced a 'pulpero' to the skin;
But he hadn't made much of that lucky win,
He'd a poor rig-out from foot to head
And a little bare saddle made it clear
He hadn't spent it on riding gear.
To Martin Fierro first of all,
He bowed as the boss of the festival,
Then he drew up a box and he sat him down,
And said, if to them it was all the same,
That 'Picardia' was all the name
He'd prefer just then to own;
He hoped they'd humour that harmless whim,
And if they'd allow him to tell his tale,
To know at the end they shouldn't fail,
The name that his father had given him;
Then on the spot he took the guitar,
And cleared his throat for song,
He tuned the strings, and he thrummed a bar,
And sang out clear and strong.

XXI

PICARDIA

I'M going to tell you the story here
  Of a luckless wanderer,
    And first of all I'd have you know
    The start and root of all my woe:
I lost my mother before my eyes
  Knew how to weep for her.

Forlorn and naked I was left,
  My father I never knew;
    Like an eggling fall'n from a scattered nest,
    I could find in the world no help nor rest,
And here and there for a bite of food
  On my half-fledged wings I flew.

It's either because of the Army laws,
  Or the lawless frontier-press;
    No matter which is more to blame,
    In the harm they do they're both the same;
They sweep the land and leave a band
  Of orphans in wretchedness.

I might have a better tale to tell,
  Had not evil fate forestalled me.
    'Inocencia' was my mother's name,
    Yet I have to admit to my lasting shame,
That because of my rogueries very soon
  o'Picardia' people called me.

The first job I had was with a man
Who owned a flock of sheep,
But all day long from morn to night
It was scoldings and whackings, left and right,
And not even a sack to rest my back
In the shed where I used to sleep.

At the faintest ray of the dawning day
He routed me out in a trice;
All the livelong day I rounded those sheep
Till back at night I could scarcely creep,
oAnd the sheep that died, the caranchos ate,
But I paid for—at market price.

You can easily guess that in such distress
I laid for a get-away;
Well down on my ears I pressed my hat,
And I trailed with the troop of an acrobat,
That happened to pass through our patch of grass
oOn the road to Santa Fé.

The boss of the show, who walked the rope,
Soon took me under his wing.
On my feet I was always neat and quick
And I didn't take long to learn the trick,
But a joke they played on me one day made
Me throw up the circus-ring.

In a tight-rope dance, it happened by chance
That my pants got somehow torn;
The crowd down below began to laugh
And I missed my foot at their jeers and chaff,
I never came nearer breaking my neck
Since the day that I was born.

So once again like a straggled calf,
 At random I turned to roam;
  I wandered round for a week or two,
  Then I thought I'd go back to the parts I knew,
When some ladies who said they were aunts of mine
 Said they'd take me and give me a home.

I had never heard a single word
 Of those relatives, I'll swear,
  But I didn't stop to hum and hem,
  They were good old souls and I took to them,
Though greater prayer-mumblers in my life,
 I've never met anywhere.

At the very first knell of the matin bell
 They began their religious labours.
  A hundred rosaries they'd recite,
  And they went through the calendar every night,
When they gathered in there, for collective prayer,
 The wives of all the neighbours.

I've never forgot how it fell to my lot
 To interrupt their devotions;
  They would make me go on my knees to pray,
  And word for word after them to say,
But it seemed that the devil was at my ear,
 And muddled up all my notions.

It must have been Satan tempting me
 And my slips I had to pay;
  I remember the drubbings I went through
  That left my sides all black and blue,
Because I couldn't say after my aunt
 o'Articulos de la Fé.'

Where I knelt to pray, a mulatto girl
    Used to come and kneel hard by.
      A native of Santa Fé was she,
        Like a guardian angel she stuck to me,—
As game and shapely a bit of goods
    As ever hit your eye.

'Begin,'—my aunt said,—'after me:
    "Articulos de la Fé." '
      I was thinking of something else just then
        I could only gape like a pip-sick hen,
Then I looked at the brownie and stuttered out
 o'Articulos de Santa Fé.'

My aunt landed out with the round-arm clout,
    I'd already seen on the way;
      I knew my mistake was ridiculous,
        So I started again with 'Articulos'—
Then the wench caught my eye, and before I could shy,
    I added:—'de Santa Fé.'

The whole day long, I prayed clear and strong,
    No trouble it came to be;
      But when the vespers time came round,
        I could hardly get out a single sound,
Which is why I say, that to make me stray,
    The devil was tempting me.

One stormy night she gave me a fright,
   oI shook like I'd caught the 'chucho';
      To look at her made me all perspire,
      Her eyes were like balls of fizzy fire,
o'San Camilo' said my aunt to me,
      And I gave her back: 'San Camilucho.'

One spiked my ribs with her elbow-bone,
   One kicked my other sides;
      Though I think I've got one of the tenderest hearts,
      I'm also tender in other parts,
I wished them in hell with all their prayers,
      For mouldy old bones-and-hides.

Another time when that darkie girl
   Began rolling her eyes at me—
      When I woke up again and could understand;
      Each aunt had a tuft of my hair in hand—
We'd been asking the 'extirpation' then
      'Of every heresy.'

Said my aunt to me: 'Of all heresies,
   Pray now for the extirpation.'
      I was thinking: My God I'll get the gripes
      If with more of this nonsense you stuff my tripes.
My tongue got in knots, and 'of heresies'
      oI prayed 'for the "entripation." '

Without a sound they fell on me,
　Those wiry old termagants;
　　I dreamt months after that luckless date
　　Of the heresies we would extirpate,
But every night I prayed for the quick
　Extirpation of all my aunts.

And rosary after rosary
　And pattering creeds and prayers,
　　Day by day and night after night,
　　Here and there and left and right;
Till at last I trailed for the plains again
　Fed up with those fool affairs.

XXII

THE GAMBLER

AS poor as a church-mouse I went off,
　　For a time I was destitute;
　　When at last I got some work to do,
　　God knows what rumpus began to brew;
oI said to myself: 'Crane,—make for home
　　Though you hop on a single foot.'

The years I'd passed in my wanderings
　　Full many had been, and hard;
　　The only capital I had got
　　Were the lessons those years to me had taught.
When I got back home they called me up
　　To serve in the National Guard.

I could do what I liked with a pack of cards,
    And gambling was my flair,
        I very soon fixed up a ramp
        With a tavern-keeper—a bit of a scamp—
In that partnership we were chip and chip,
    And we each went share and share.

With practice I was a regular dab
    ○At sanding, or stacking a deck;
        In the box like new he'd stow them away
    ○Till we saw our chance to flap a jay;
When you know in the deal where the honours fall,
    You needn't punt on spec.

I figure they make a big mistake
    Who put their trust in luck;
        ○The man that's flash at the bunco-game
        ○Will rake the pot on them just the same;
They may count they win if they save their skin,
    With no feathers left to pluck.

With a wide-awake partner that knows the books,
    ○Nimble fives, and a salted pack,
        You can earn a good living in dollars and cents
        And silver buckles and ornaments;
To take a hand in a friendly round
    ○A pigeon you'll seldom lack.

There's many a trick the expert knows,
    That no one can call a crime,
        There's few that know, when they risk their wads,
        ○What a sharp can do with a pack of broads;
○With a well-placed bonnet to tip the code
    He'll rook them every time.

Just let them see, as if carelessly,
  oIn the lay-out, the card that's 'gate,'
    They see a cinch and they stake their life,
    And they run right onto the point of your knife,
Because of course you change the card
  As soon as they take the bait.

At the game of 'monte' don't forget
  Precautions however slight.
    Get your fingers well set before you begin,
    It's with them, not the cards, you've got to win;
And see that you take a seat that's low,
  Where you give your back to the light.

When you cut the cards, see you give the shade;
  Get in the way of the light;
    As soon as the game is well commenced
    Suit your play to the man you're up against;
Keep your eyes well skinned—the game of cards
  Is a game that needs practised sight.

The other fellow may open his too,
  But eyes are no good to fools;
    oJust give him rope, and get in your work
    When you see you can grass him with the jerk;
There isn't a dub, but thinks he's a dab,
  With the cards, once he knows the rules.

There's lots of beetle-heads about
  That trust to simple luck;
    When they're flush you can pluck them as you please,
    oThey even lose on aces and threes,
All you need to do is to lead them on,
  And once they plunge they're stuck.

The fool won't win though to Santa Rita
 He prays for a solid week;
  At the table an old hand spots a jay
  As soon as he ever sits down to play,
And with me they hadn't the ghost of a chance
 Not even at hide-and-seek.

At 'nines' and other games of skill
 My luck is really funny;
  As soon as to deal my turn I get,
  There doesn't seem any help for it,—
oTop-shuffle the deck and shift the cut—
 And it's simply taking their money.

oAt 'truco' I soon had the best at bay
 Whenever they played with me.
  If I happen to need a trick or two
  I can keep in my hand, as if stuck with glue,
Whatever I fancy—the ace of spades,
 A high-pair or a three.

To sit at a table to lose your stakes
 Is a game I don't understand.
  If you're going to bet on the turn of a card,
  Wake up your wits and keep thinking hard,—
Whenever at 'monte' we played a round,
 The barkeep would take a hand.

Every single card of a well-stacked deck
    I can carry pat in my head.
        From the moment they start to tumble out,
        I can follow them round without a doubt;
I know the trick that's lost or won,
    As soon as a card is led.

It's very true that at such games
    One's sometimes in a fix.
        But I'm not such a fool at that artful play
        As ever to give myself away;
They can check up the discard when they like,
    Without finding out my tricks.

oWith 'high-men' or 'low-men' I landed them
    If they tried their luck at dice;
        The ones that were flash to the boney-game
        I'd lighten their belts for, just the same;
oBy ringing the changes or pulling a bluff
    Right under their very eyes.

oAt 'taba' too, I could beat a few;
    At billiards I was a dandy.
        And to cut it short, I'll only add
        That my craze for gaming got so bad
I'd play with the boys at knuckle-bones
    If nothing else was handy.

I'll not deny it's a low-down game,
And leaves a bad taste behind.
For every sharp on the gambling lay
Is on the look-out to trap a jay,
And say what you like, it's a robbery
To play with a man that's blind.

And I'll tell you this—it's not advice,
But just what I learnt I'm giving:
I'm sorry now for the time I lost,
For all I won wasn't worth the cost,
And it's harder to learn a vice like that
Than to work for an honest living.

XXIII

THE DISTRICT OFFICER

AN Italian peddlar that went about
  With a harpist for a pard,
  Fell into our net like a simpleton;
  I made him burst at 'thirty-one,'
I let him see what was coming out—
  As if I was off my guard.

The man had been acting the fool with me,
  And I gave him bluff for bluff.
    When he thought the stakes were in his bag,
    He found himself up to his neck in the quag,
oFor Santa Lucia blinded him
  And I raked in all his stuff.

At the loss of his traps you should have seen
  What a terrible fuss he made;
    o'Ma gañao con picardia,' he cried,
    As he mopped his tears and sobbed and sighed,
While in a poncho I bundled up
  Every stick of his stock-in-trade.

He was rid of his load, but he didn't seem
  To be pleased with the deal he'd driven,
    Perhaps he fell for an easy prey
    Because he played cards on the Sabbath day;
For that kind of gringo hasn't got
  A patron Saint in heaven.

But little I gained for all I got.
   The devil was on my track,
      In the shape of a district officer,
      An ugly pug-nosed customer,
Because of his pug they nicknamed him
   oThe 'Ñato'—behind his back.

He soon came round to collect the fine
   That he said I had to pay;
      I'd broken the law, he'd have me know,
      And by rights to jail I ought to go;
The end of it was, he took one half
   Of all I'd won at play.

The way the man high-handed me,
   Fair rubbed me on the raw;
      I had lifted the peddlar's pack, it's true,
      By certain artful tricks I knew,
But he was simply plundering me
   By threatening me with the law.

They said for a time, because of some crime,
   Round those parts he could scarcely stir,
      Until a friend got him out of disgrace
      By fixing the Judge that handled the case;
And shortly after he got a job
   As a full-blown officer.

He was always as busy as could be,
   Going the rounds of the section.
      Though a single 'bad-man' he never caught,
      A pack-horse back he always brought,
Piled up with hens and ducks and lambs,
   Like a regular collection.

An abuse that gets to such a pitch,
 Is just a barefaced crime;
  Month after month he worked that lay,
  Until the neighbours commenced to say,
'This "ñato" rascal has revived
 The tithes of the olden-time.'

He fancied himself on the guitar,
 And a singer furthermore,
  On the counter I found him sitting one night,
  Strumming and singing with all his might,
∘And I said to him, 'Co ... mo ... quiando
 Con ganas de oir un cantor ...'

The 'ñato' gave me a look as if
 He could tear me limb from limb,
  But he let on he didn't understand
  And went on howling to beat the band,
But I needn't tell that he knew quite well
 I was sick of the sight of him.

At a neighbour's house I met him once—
 I was dying to make him ratty.
  To pick a quarrel with him I'd vowed;
  ∘So, 'Ña ... to ... ribia,' I called out loud,
'Make sure the water is at the boil,
 Before you brew the "maté."'

He was the 'do-all' of the Judge—
 The joke made him prancing mad;
  He up and answered me on the spot:
  'When I get the chance you'll catch it hot;
You'll be scalded well when I'm done with you,
 And you'll know who I am, my lad.'

And over a woman the quarrel got worse,
When once it was fairly started,
The 'ñato' was after her, plain to see,
A buxom, strapping wench was she,
A girl like a heifer, as people say,
And very tender-hearted.

I came on her one day kneading dough,—
She was something to admire!
I said to her: 'It would give me pleasure
To assist you, madam, in some small measure,
oSo if you'll allow me, I'll hand you the bones
When you need them to feed the fire.'

The 'ñato' was draping himself around
Like a lazy, lounging, sloven;
She saw there was trouble ready-brewed,
And to keep it from spilling if she could,
She answered me: 'If you bring the bones
Put them over there, by the oven.'

From that day the fat was in the fire,
All over that incident.
He didn't trouble to hide it more
That he looked at me as an open sore,
And he only wanted to find his chance
To get me some punishment.

I saw he was rankling for my hide,
And the waiting made him fretsome,
The slightest chance he wouldn't lose,
To jerk me up in his wily noose;
And the true man only keeps his life
As long as the traitor lets him.

The craftiest beast gets trapped at last
 The wildest is tamed or shorn;
   So I thought it best after that affair
   Not to move too far outside my lair,
oLike the 'San Ramon' that's put back on the shelf
 Once the baby is safely born.

XXIV

THE POLLS

THERE were two or three times, by the skin
of my teeth
    I scarcely got away;
He toadied round his boss, the Judge,
And made him the catspaw for his grudge,
Till at last he caught me off my guard
    At the polls on election-day.

I remember that day there were several lists
    Filled up with different names,
        There was bound to be trouble it seemed to me,
        For the parties did nothing but disagree,
And the talk went round that the Judge, to win
    Was up to some dirty games.

When the crowd was in, the 'ñato' came
    The polls to inaugurate;
        By way of an opening address
        He said we would land in a pretty mess,
If every voter was going to vote
    For a different 'candilate.'

He grabbed 'at my list, but at grabbing games
    He found I was quick and tricky;
        I cheated his snatch with turn and twist
        And he roared at me: 'You anarchist!
You've got to vote for the list I've brought,
    That's approved by the "Comicky." '

To be used like that, and in public too,
  With my grain fair disagrees;
    And seeing as how when you once get riled
    It's hard to lie down and fizz out mild,
I said: 'Whoever your boss may be,
  I'll vote as I dam well please.

'At the gaming-board or the ballot-box
  I'm as good as anyone.
    If I'm left alone I won't make no row,
    But I'm not taking orders anyhow;
And it gets my goat, if my card or my vote
  A man lays his finger on.'

With no more words, with naked swords
  The police fell on me quick;
    I saw it was just a put-up job,
    So I didn't offer to fight that mob,
They were only waiting to see me draw,
  And my last they'd have made me kick.

They caught me off my guard that day,—
  The 'ñato' and his mates—
    Since then I'm up to such-like tricks
    And I'll meddle no more with politics,
For I went for a canter in the stocks
  All over those 'candilates.'

It wasn't because I was scared of them
  Those wrongs I had to bear.
    That day at the polls had set me wise,
    And taken the blinkers off my eyes;
Like a dog with a trammel at its neck
  I saw they had got us there.

Since those elections, things got worse,
    And more mixed up and shady;
        A fankle of string without end or middle,—
        I'd like to have Justice solve this riddle:
How she rides on the pillion of every rogue,
    And yet keeps her name as a lady?

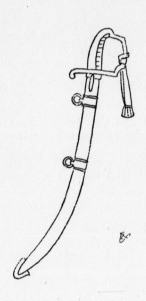

XXV

THE CONTINGENT

O N the heels of the ballot, before the crowd
    To their homes had a chance to clear,
      A notice to every man they sent
        To wait till they drafted a contingent;
The army again was in need of men
      To defend the far frontier.

The gauchos didn't wait for more,
  They scattered far and wide.
    To fetch them in the troop went out,
    And scoured the whole place round about;
And a few more wretches they gathered up
  That hadn't had time to hide.

The 'ñato' high-handed the wretched bunch,
  Said he: 'They're a scrappy lot;
    I rounded them up without a sound,
    They hadn't a chance with me, they found;
My orders were to bring back with me
  Every beast that two legs has got.'

The Commandant fixed them with his eye
  As if he had thunder-struck them;
    'God help us all' to myself I said,
    And I tried to look like a dunderhead;
He gave them a blessing one by one,
  And down on the list he stuck them.

He roared at a nigger: 'Come over here;
  Stop playing the lamb now—"Shun!"
    You're the damndest rogue in all the place,
    To pack you off is an act of grace,
So down in the army draft you go,
  I'll give you number One.'

      To another.
'You leave your family without a cent
  To provide their necessities,
    You go with other women, you rake,
    You'll be better gone for everyone's sake,
We'll teach you out in the frontier post
  To know what your duty is.'

To another.

'A fine lot of trouble you put us to,
　　When we want you in to vote
　　　You're always too busy with other affairs,
　　　And you go round aping your betters' airs,
You're a "disinsubordinate" perky rogue,
　　So your name on the roll I'll note.'

To another.

'I'd like to know for just how long
　　You've been loafing round this camp;
　　　How many times, just tell me too,
　　　Have you come when the Judge has cited you?
I've never set eyes on your face before,
　　You must be a proper scamp.'

To another.

'Here's another brawler that day and night
　　Hangs round the pulperías,
　　　The greatest ranter I ever saw,
　　　To stir up the people against the law,—
We've got a cure in the frontier troop
　　For all such fool ideas.'

To another.

'Since I packed the last batch out of here
　　I've hardly seen your face,
　　　Though your name is down on the voters' rolls
　　　We've never got you to the polls,
Whenever we send to call you in
　　You slip off to some other place.'

To another.

'You're always in clover, so it seems,
    You've no lawful wage or trade,
        You've dodged the vote and you've dodged the rank
        I'll put a stop to your roguish pranks,
So off you go—for round these parts
    It's mischief enough you've made.'

To another.

'Hand over your papers now, you there!
    I'll take them and put them by,
        You won't need none for a goodish while,
        And when you get back they'll be on my file,
Like that, if you make for a get-away
    We'll soon raise a hue-and-cry.'

To another.

'You're a rascally rebel; you've got me tired
    With your smirkings and grimacings,
        You got an exception, didn't you?
        And you think you're excepted from voting too?
There's no exception goes down with me;
    I'll soon put you through your facings!'

And because of this, or because of that,
    Not a single one he rejected;
        The whole bang lot, without missing one,
        He polished them off, every mother's son,
Until in a corner of the room
    He had them all collected.

And there their sisters and their wives,
　　And their mothers set up a crying;
　　　　With sobs and prayers they gathered round,
　　　　While with bitter tears their eyes were drowned,
But love can't cure a grief like that,
　　And it isn't patched up by sighing.

It ain't no use for a mother there,
　　For her darling son to blub;
　　　　There isn't nobody cares a hoot,
　　　　If a man leaves his woman destitute;
You've got to shut up, or as sure as fate
　　They split you through the hub.

The women folk ask for help perhaps,
　　From some of the landed neighbours.
　　　　When a woman wants help, most men are sly,
　　　　And they never run but they start to fly;
So often the poor things only get
　　Worse trouble for all their labours.

There were some trailed off to ask the Judge
　　To let their men go free;
　　　　The Judge was an old hand at the game,
　　　　And he wasn't going to take the blame,
He said: 'I'm real sorry at all your worry,
　　But it's nothing to do with me.'

They still hung round; and when more came up
　　And their prayers they began renewing,
　　　　To clinch the matter he said to them:
　　　　'Like Pilate, the Judge of Jerusalem,
I wash my feet of the whole affair,
　　This is all the Commandant's doing.'

To see the poor wretches wander off,
    The hardest heart might harrow,
        There were mothers with two or three babes, or
            more,—
        A pack behind, and a pack before,—
With never a home to turn them to,
    And as penniless as a sparrow.

What lair are they going to find, I thought,
    To shelter their nakedness;
        Who's going to blame them I'd like to know
        If they curse the gang that runs this show?
There's a peck of trouble brewing here,
    Among all this wretchedness.

XXVI

'PICARDIA' TELLS HIS NAME

WHEN my turn came round I said to myself:
 'I'm in for it now, I suppose.'
  I hadn't done anything very bad,
  I can't explain the fright I had,
I had Jesus' name on the tip of my tongue,
 As the common saying goes.

He called me a gambler, a good-for-nought,
 A shame to the mother that bore me;
  Since I came to the district, so he'd heard,
  I'd been buzzing about like a humming-bird,
That I was a bandit without a doubt,
 As my father had been before me.

A man may have a vice or two,—
 That nobody denies,—
  But it doesn't help matters a little bit,
  To try and shame him because of it;
I guessed that the 'ñato' was the one
 That had put the Commandant wise.

I began to wonder what he meant,
 And I guess I had good cause—
  When he called my father a bandit, flat,
  It seemed he was telling me by that,
That he'd known my father; while even I
 Had never known who he was.

I pricked my ears and I scratched around,
    Though at first it seemed no use,
        I vowed to Jesus that I'd reform,
        If he'd show me a trail where the scent was warm;
And at last I found I was the son
    Of the gallant Sergeant Cruz.

The name wasn't new, for though years had passed,
    Round those parts the tale was spread,
        How Cruz one night in the police patrol
        Had played his life like a valiant soul
To defend a man he was sent to take
    And bring in alive or dead.

I pray the Father of all to keep
  My father's soul in glory;
    He sent me his blessing when he died,
    In the wilderness by his comrade's side,
And I bless him too for leaving me
  The heritage of his story.

From that day on I took my oath
  I'd live inside the laws;
    I can look any man in the eye and say
    I've made a clean break with yesterday,
And I'm living now on the fair and square,
  Since I knew who my father was.

A son shouldn't live on his father's fame
  Till he's squandered it all away,
    If you don't show respect for your father's blood
    You'll soon have his name all messed with mud,
And you'll get your fill of grief and ill
  Some sorrowful settling-day.

To mend my ways for my father's sake
  For months was my one idea;
    I wiped my past out bit by bit,
    Till at last I was quit of it every whit,
Save the last rag-end I can't shed or mend:
  The name of 'Picardia.'

You'll save yourself trouble if your name
  Stands well with your fellow men;
    Take this advice from one who knows
    And paid it dear with pains and woes:
It's a heap more easy to smudge your name
  Than to wipe it clean again.

XXVII

WHAT HE SAW ON THE FRONTIER

IT wasn't by rights they drafted me
For the ranks—but Fate is hard;
And for many a year on the far frontier
I served in the Border-guard.

The 'ñato' had had it in for me,
And he got his chance at last;
And by his craft in the army draft
He trapped me firm and fast.

And in the hell of a frontier-post
   Full bitter I had to sup,
Because that Jack-in-office there
   I had rubbed the wrong way up.

I won't start harping on the wrongs
   And the pains I suffered yonder;
They've been told so often that one forgets
   They once were a nine-days' wonder.

It's always the same damned wretchedness
   And the same grind, day by day,
The same routine and the same fatigue,
   And the same not a cent of pay.

Always covered with filthy rags
   Or bare to the very pelt,
With never a clout to patch your bags
   Or a red-cent in your belt.

Make the best of it, without togs or pay,
   Though you stretch your muzzle out;—
If you can't get the skilly down your throat,—
   Just don't—and you go without.

If you answer pert, or perk your comb,
   Or move a bit slow and lazy,
They give you a nine-day staking-out
   That leaves you plumb dam crazy.

Among the whole ragamuffin lot
   A 'peso' you couldn't find;
It's the Army way to keep the pay
   A couple of years behind.

They're always talking of what it costs,
    That the Border's a sink of money,
But I never set eyes on a single 'real'
    Which to say the least is funny.

They threaten and drub you right and left,
    And here and there they harry you,
And you don't even know what kind of face
    God has given to the 'Comisario.'

When he comes to review, he's off like a shot
    Before he can well begin,
He's almost as quick as a 'Will-o-the-wisp'
    At popping out and in.

And—what seemed to me like a put-up job—
    It always turned out this way:
It was always for men that had gone back home
    That he brought the arrears of pay.

It couldn't come out a bit more pat
    If they did it by rule and score,
When I came, the pay had just arrived
    For the draft that had gone before.

You'd think they've a warrant, the way they search
    For the ones that aren't there,
While the ragged bunch that have just come in
    Can perish for all they care.

Till what with the hell they serve you there,
    You either run away,
Or they make you croak, or they turn you off
    Without a cent of pay.

That's the way they make the Border pie,
    And who's going to interfere
And raise a hand for the gaucho's rights
    Away on the far frontier?

When they call them in to drill they look so ill
    They seem next door to dying,
And their flapping rags like little flags
    Behind their backs are flying.

There's nothing to do till their time is up
    But simply to grin and bear,
And when they're discharged they're bundled out
    With hardly a clout to wear.

If they've given them a stitch or a scrap of gear
    They call it in again,
Poncho and bridle and saddle and horse,
    They strip from them there and then.

When the wretched crowd for their native parts
    Are ready to hit the track,
The luckiest one among the lot
    Has scarcely a shirt to his back.

A sadder sight I've seldom seen,
    It's clean beyond belief—
The best rigged-out of that ragged rout
    Is like parsley without the leaf.

It was only the other day I saw
    A bunch go off together
Almost mother-naked, to pad the hoof
    For home in the winter weather.

You wouldn't believe the skinflint lot
   That run the show out there—
Not an old crocked nag for the homeward trail
   To that wretched crew will spare.

They treat you worse than an infidel,
   You'd think you had done some crime;
And to cap it all, not a paper you get
   To show that you've served your time.

Without a cent, without a discharge—
   You can guess just how it feels:
Fair game for every crimping-gang
   That can lay you by the heels.

And what became of your goods and gear,
   Just enquire—if you're indiscreet—
Your wife sold the lot for what she got,
   To buy her a bite to eat.

They all play into each other's hands
   And it's all in the dirty game,
You'll come off bad if you go getting mad
   Or start in to make a claim.

If you make for a ranch and beg a bite—
   What else can a poor man do?
They call you a landlouper or a tramp,
   And set the police after you.

It's good high time it seems to me
   The Government scrapped all that;
If the Army wants men, let it hire them, then,—
   And stop playing mouse-and-cat.

Of the learning writ in the townsmen's books
　　My head ain't exactly crammed,—
But I tell you this: if you're born on a ranch
　　You're born as good as damned.

And I don't think it's going too far to say
　　Since I'm making comparisons,
That the country's a mother that doesn't care
　　One rap for her wretched sons.

They die like dogs in the great wide wastes
　　Where the Border never sleeps,
Or like bullocks they break the stubborn plain
　　For the crops that another reaps.

And I'll add this more: it gets me sore
　　How time and time again
Men prate of their country, but have no time
　　To waste on their countrymen.

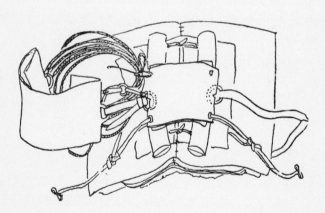

XXVIII

THE RATIONS

THIS tongue of mine goes wagging on
There's a devil in it, I fear—
I'll tell you some of the pretty ways
They have on the far frontier.

I'm well aware that over there
The best way to get along
Is to meet with a shrug or a smiling mug
What hits you—right or wrong.

If you haven't a mattress for your back
With what you can get, be happy;
The cat always curls up by the fire,
Which shows he's a knowing chappie.

By this, if you get me, you'll understand
   You'll miss many a nasty jar
If you don't protest, but just make the best
   Of things, as you find they are.

A scurvy time I had of it,
   Like the rest of those wretched men,
Till they made me an officer's orderly,
   And I found myself better then.

The pains you bear drive you near despair,
   You're as lean as a starving hound;
But there's always lashings in the mess
  oOf the crowd that pack braid around.

From that time on I lost my fear
   I was fated to die of want,
I managed to worm myself slyly in
   At the side of the Adjutant.

He was always buried in piles of books,
   And very much on his perch;
They said it was cram for some exam
   He was taking, to join the church.

Though they pulled his leg, he didn't get wild
   Nor even lay complaint;
He had big wide-open staring eyes
   Like the eyes of a holy Saint.

He always slept in a regular bed,—
    I thought it a funny whim—
oHe was nick-named 'La Bruja'; God knows why,
    And the men loathed the sight of him.

It was easy to see that love of work
    Wasn't numbered among his passions,
For all the duty he ever did
    Was to give out the daily rations.

You can easy guess when I joined his mess
    I was charmed with my new position,
And the very first day he took me out
    To help him with his commission.

The rank and file must have their smile—
    They're always in joking feather—
They smacked their lips and wiped their mouths,
    When they saw us go off together.

And they said as they sat around the fires:
    'We're in for a feast, you bet,
With a brace like "Bruja" and "Picardia"
    Fine rations we're going to get!'

I didn't do badly for myself
    For my boss knew all the tricks;
I'll tell you now, in the Army how
    These little things they fix.

They said 'La Bruja' had fixed a ramp
    With the Government purveyor
And took all the throw-backs—may be so—
    For he wasn't asleep, I'll swear.

That furthermore in the quantity,
    He bit off another whack;
That of every ration on the list,
    The rogue kept one half back.

And of course he covered up his tracks,
    As a knowing fellow ought,
By signing the bill in proper form,
    For the things that he never got.

There are tales like that in every camp,
    In a score of styles and fashions,
They may be true—I'm just telling you,
    How we dealt with those famous rations.

'La Bruja' loaded the vittles up
    And checked how much was less,
Then we toted the lot until we got
    To the door of the Major's mess.

They took out their whack in the Major's mess
    And they didn't knock nothing off it;
It was only fair that a margin there
    Should be skimmed, by way of profit.

The rations then passed to the Company,
    The Commandant there received 'em;
And nobody tallied what he took out,
    If they had, it would sure have peeved him.

When they'd helped themselves, our lightened loads
    We toted off once more;
And then to the Officer of the week
    We handed the remanant o'er.—
Do one good turn and get another,
o'Ka me, ka thee' saves heaps of bother.

To the sergeant then he passed them on,
    But before they left his grip,
Of everything that he fancied most
    He took a thumping dip.

I'd never get through if I told to you
    Every step of that execution—
The Sergeant next puts the corporal
    In charge of the distribution.

'First come first served' is the corporal's rule,
    And he's number One—don't doubt it,—
He does himself proud, before all the crowd,
    And he makes no bones about it.

So many rake-offs those rations stand,
    When they halt every little while,
That there's not much left when at last they get
    Within reach of the rank and file.

It's as spare a meal as you get at mass,
    oAnd I tell you, compañero,
It takes three or four, and sometimes more
    oTo make up one poor 'puchero.'

They tell you everything's done 'O.K.'
    As per Army regulation,
But to know you're starved by rule, I'll say
    Ain't much of a consolation.

I've seen some days—I'm not kidding you,
    Or talking tall or funny—
There was nothing at all but the scraps and crumbs
    That had stuck in the empty gunny.

And the tale they tell to explain that hell
   Where they drive you nearly silly,
Is, the Government doesn't send the cash
   To pay for the soldier's skilly.

I'm not heading any enquiry here
   As to that, you may start to bet;
If they say so, I guess it's Jake with me,—
   I don't learn; but I don't forget.

The vilest treatment they serve you out;
   You've just got to bear, and grin,—
You're whacked with a stick when you're out of the ranks
   And whacked with a sword when you're in.

The uniforms are another hell—
   I've never seen nothing rummer;
The summer ones come in the winter-time,
   And the winter ones in summer.

The why and wherefore's got me beat,
   Though I'd very much like to know.
If you ask, they tell you the powers that be,
    Have fixed it up just so.

It ain't no use, to try shaking loose,
   When Fate's got you on her line;
The gaucho must pay by getting killed,
   For being an Argentine.

   It seems to be his destiny
    From his birth to live accursed;
As a wag once said: 'If they've got to be killed,
   It's better to strip them first.'

They never get any forrader
    At stopping that rotten game;
Though the bosses change the thing goes on
    Every wretched bit the same.

And you'll find some men such a bad-biled lot
    That they'll say, without going round it,
If you want to soften the gaucho's hide,
    With a cudgel you've got to pound it.

There's nothing to do but drink your cup
    Though you shy at the bitter flavour;
It seems the gaucho's always got
    A pile of sins to pay for.

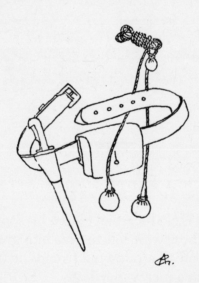

XXIX

IN WHICH A NEGRO SINGER APPEARS

WHEN 'Picardia' closed his song,
There were lots to give him greeting,
And all around old friends he found—
It sure was a merry meeting.
But it happened that Chance that's never far off,
Seeing so many whites together,
Saw fit to bring to their gathering
A bird of a darker feather.

A nigger he was, that preened himself
As a regular top-hole singer,
You could see by his cheek that to open his beak
He didn't aim to linger.
(You can always tell a man that's bent
On starting up some kind of argument.)
He sauntered across and sat him down
As if he felt mighty grand,
And on the guitar rang an opening bar
That told of a practised hand.
He was all tricked up in a flash rig-out,
And as if to leave nobody long in doubt
Of what he had come for, he started there
To clear his throat and to hum an air.
It was plain he was pecking at Fierro's comb,
By his jaunty cocksure manner;
He couldn't have made it a bit more clear
If he'd carried it on a banner:
Nor was Fierro slow to take him up,
His strings in turn he rang;
While the company listened, he started off,
And these were the words they sang:—

XXX

MARTIN FIERRO

AS long as there's sound in the strumming strings
   And my hand hasn't lost its cunning,
     You won't find me slow to toe the scratch
    And hold my own in a singing-match,
And if I'm not first at the winning-post
   It won't be for want of running.

Let him open his ear who wants to hear,
   And the gossipers take a vacation;
     I'll ask you folks to pardon me
    If I make any slips, for it's plain to see
That no one's perfectly free from faults
   Who can't withstand temptation.

It's custom to call a singer good
   If he betters the worst of the batch,
     And when two songsters get together,
    Though they mayn't be birds of the finest feather,
It's up to the pair their gifts to air
   By holding a singing-match.

One shouldn't be slow at giving his show
   At the proper time and occasion.
     If he isn't trying to pull a bluff,
    The first time of asking's quite enough,
And there's lots that like to be buttered up
   With a heap of fool persuasion.

When I was young, sweet songs I sung—
  The phrase has been used before—
    But luck has many an impish whim,
    Misfortune dogged me and turned me grim,
Ah times agone! since those days on,
  I sing of my sorrows sore.

Those happy years of my careless youth
  I'll try to recall to mind,
    The trials that beset me, the pains I met,
    For a time at least I'll just forget,
Let the strings resound! I'll sing a round
  With any that feels inclined.

Tune up, tune up! and all night we'll sing
  To the lilt of the ringing gut;
    The company's waiting; we're both in fettle,
    Come sing with me and I'll test your mettle,
The strings we'll thrum till the morning's come,
  And the candles burn to the butt.

And the singer bold that wants to hold
  A singing-match with me,—
    No matter how clever and smart he feels
    He needn't expect to see my heels;
We'll start right now and take turn and turn,
  Till the blink of the dawn we see.

And we'll carry right on till the daylight's gone,—
  To a tee it'll suit my ways;
    I mind me well when my years were young
    That many a time all night I've sung;
There were fancy top-notch warblers then,
  Like you don't meet nowadays.

And if anyone fret at the pace I set
  Or can't follow my galopings,
    Or once he's in, doesn't aim to win
    I tell him straight: he'd better begin
To leave the guitar to his betters, and play
  On a sponge, with woollen strings.

The Nigger.

There's many that are, on the guitar,
  More clever and light and larky;
    I'll only say I'm a middling player,
      But I'm sure plumb glad heav'n's heard my prayer
And a singer I've met that seems all set
  To try-out this humble darkie.

Though I'm black of blee, don't think less of me,
  I guess I just can't remove it.
    I've got civil ways and I know my place,
      You can smile if you like at my darky face,
I've got something white in my make-up too;
  And here are my teeth to prove it.

My mother dear, ten sons she bore
  And nine of them middling good;
    oI was number Ten, which is why, maybe,
      That Providence always favoured me.
They say the tenth egg of a laying hen
  Is the biggest of all the brood.

A warm-hearted race are the black-of-face,
  Though they don't spread the news around;
    There's nothing to beat how they stick together
      And they stick the closer the worse the weather,
oThey're like the 'macá,' for under its wing
  Its chickens are always found.

But since I was grown, I've been on my own,
  For myself I've always fended;
    I've always roamed like a bird as free,
      And every tree is a home for me,
All the learning I've got, by a priest was taught
  Whose class I once attended.

I know as well as the man next door
　　Why the clouds are thunder-riven,
　　　　The months of the year; and a thing that's rummer—
　　　　Why winter comes on the heels of summer;
And I know the way they gather up
　　The waters that fall from Heaven.

I know what they hide in the earth's inside
　　When you get right to the middle,
　　　　The caverns deep where the gold is found,
　　　　And the iron, miles underneath the ground,
And the flaming volcanoes rage and roar,—
　　And many another riddle.

I know how the shining fish are born
　　Way down on the ocean's bottom;
　　　　I know the trees how they spring and grow,
　　　　And why the winds whistle when they blow,
And many things that the whites don't know,
　　This darkie's wits have taught him.

I'll pull or let go, go fast or slow,
　　Swop knocks, if you're bent on knocking,
　　　　I guess I won't keep him waiting long,
　　　　Who challenges me to a round of song;
It's silly to ask if a man is lame,
　　You'll know, if you watch him walking.

And if my foot, out of place I've put,
　　By showing you here my figure,
　　　　And airing my voice before I was bade,
　　　　Please pardon me; and I'll only add:
There's no defect so almighty big
　　That someone can't find a bigger.

In every song it won't take folks long
   To find something odd to pick on;
      Does it matter a bit if the singer's black?
      Just listen! Don't snigger behind his back.
The fool may pick up a grain of wit,
   And the wisest their wits may slicken.

A brow like coal covers sense and soul,
   And may have good wits for lining;
      Just give me a show, and hark to me,
      And don't get cross if you don't agree;
The night's black too, but the light gets through
   Where the big bright stars are shining.

So fire away and sound my wits,
   You won't find me slow or surly;
      Ask what you like but please overlook,
      If my answers don't sound like a book,
∘In letters I don't know 'J' from 'O'
   They're both so curly-wurly.

Martin Fierro.
Come on then darkie; don't jib or shy,
   In view you're so mighty wise;
      You've got the hook well down, I feel,
      So answer me right off the reel,
While the beat you ring on the sounding string;
   What song is the song of the skies?

The Nigger.
They say God fashioned the black man first
   When He planned man's shape and figure,
      Yet there's some white folks so mighty proud
      Though they ask him to sing to amuse the crowd,
They don't remember he's got a name
   But only that he's a nigger.

The white man paints the devil black,
    And the black man paints him white;
        But a man by his colour ain't influenced,
        It doesn't hold for, nor yet against;
The Almighty made only one kind of man,
    Though their faces are dark or bright.

And after this opening that fits quite well
    With my present situation;
        With my spare wits the best I'll do
        In a word or two to answer you;
And I'll tell you what the song of the skies
    Is in my estimation.

The heavens sing, and weep and sigh
    Forever and evermore,
        In the silent dawn the dew they weep,
        They sing when the winds o'er the pampas sweep,
Their tears gush out when the tempests spout,
    And they chant in the thunder's roar.

Martin Fierro.

Black and white God made, but He never said
　Which one of the two was duller;
　　　He gave them all the same cross to bear,
　　　And equal woes, and the same despair,
But He also made light, and He made it white
　The better to show up colour.

There isn't no call to get personal
　Where there's been no provocation;
　　　I don't see how anyone is to blame
　　　If they call a thing by its common name,
And a present you got on your first birthday
　Can't damage your reputation.

I like them more when they don't get sore
　And start any dander-slinging,—
　　　If your head's as long as you say it is,
　　　Please clear up some more of these mysteries,
Just tell me now, what in all the world
　Is the song that the earth is singing?

The Nigger.

My wits are in want, and my skill is scant
　With such deep dark things to deal;
　　　But I'm not getting scared on account of that,
　　　Though my head is hard, I can answer pat,
For even the pebble gives off sparks
　When you strike it with the steel.

And this is the answer that I find
　In my reason's limitations;
　　　Her song is the voice of motherhood
　　　In the bearing pangs of her mighty brood,
The last death-sighs and the first birth-cries
　Of her countless generations.

Martin Fierro.

Ah darkie! I see you don't waste your pipes
  In chirpings and twitterings;
    You can do your stuff once you get a start,
    You're a man sure enough, after Fierro's heart,
And I'm not surprised; for among the birds
  It's only the cock that sings.

And seeing as how into the world
  This gift you've brought along,
    Don't sing too small, but don't sing too big,
    And don't get ruffled and lose your twig;
And quick on the spot, just tell me what
  Is the song that's the Ocean's song.

The Nigger.

If men had been meant to sing like birds
  It's a cinch they'd be born with beaks;
    To copy a gift you were born without,
    Doesn't seem very much to be proud about,
The magpie I've heard, is a wonderful bird
  But it's only the female speaks.

Come help me on now my mother-wit
  To win this match for me.
    It costs me a bit to make reply,
    But I'm not throwing up my hand, not I—
I'll tell you now, as I best know how
  The song of the Ocean-sea.

When the mighty winds o'er the ocean blow,
  The waters all round the earth
    Rise up and sing with a dreadful roar,
    Till the whole world trembles from shore to shore,
Like a beast it howls in earth's rocky bowels
  As if raging to come to birth.

Martin Fierro.
The best of your brains you'll have to rack
    This time—I'll bet my hat—
        Make chums right now with some holy Saint,
        You'll win if you are, and you'll lose if you ain't;
As well as the Sea and the Earth and Sky,
    The Night has her song—what's that?
            The Nigger.
A wary man said to a bold man once:
    'Don't gallop, there's holes around.'
        I'll answer you simply: Night murmurs low,
        Her song on the winds that come and go,
And that echoes bear from none knows where,
    That seem but the ghosts of sound.

They're the whisperings of the secret things
    That the shadows of night enclose,
        The phantom voices that haunt the ear,
        When a cry goes up in the midnight clear,
Like the muffled tone of an endless moan
    From a source that no man knows.

When the sun rises high in the eastern sky,
    The shadows seek their lairs;
        But when night comes down on the world, then hark!
        How the voices stir in the stilly dark,—
The voice of the souls of the dead and gone
    That ask us for our prayers.
            Martin Fierro.
Well answered, darkie; you're doing well,
    You've riz in my estimation.
        You've got the knack of this singing-jargon,
        And a pinch of learning into the bargain,
Not even a shadow escapes your grip
    If it serves your explanation.

But I think it's my duty to say this plain
  Before we get on with the story,
    Will you please take note, ere we go ahead,
    I'm not singing here to raise the dead;
So I'll thank you to leave in the peace of God
  The souls that have gone to glory.

And the wary man's counsel about the holes,
  Some other may serve to warn,
    It suits with a singer best I hold
    To sing out clear and strong and bold,
And now I want you to answer quick:
  Please tell me where love is born.

        The Nigger.
A riddle rare you've given me there,—
  I haven't met many such,—
    It's lots to ask from a rough ranch hand,
    But this at least I understand:
The beginning of wisdom is to know
  That one doesn't know very much.

Love's born in the bird that wings the air
  Through the sky so blue and wide,
    When it's weary of flying to and fro
    It lights on some branch; and sweet and low
It opens its bill and with many a trill
  Calls its little mate to its side.

The wild beast loves in its gloomy lair
  Far hid from the homes of men;
    It woos its mate with fearsome growls,
    And tells its love in a burst of howls,
The only song that the wild beast knows
  Is to roar and roar again.

The shining fish that swim the sea
  Have their loves, just the same as man;
    From the ocean's deeps to the skies above,
    There's nothing's got life that hasn't love;
God made them together and yoked them up,
  The day that the world began.

Martin Fierro.

Ah, cunning darkie; you've handled well
  A ticklish proposition;
    Although at first you made me smile,
    I'm respecting you now a regular pile.
And now of the thing men call the Law
  Please give me your definition.

The Nigger.

There's lots of things that the bookmen know
  Beyond my comprehension;
    Since I found that, myself, I'm not so wise,
    No learning can cause me much surprise,
And the man that at singing takes me on,
  I'm not asking for condescension.

No singer am I, expert or sly,
  Though to win this match I'm hopin',
    But when to my turn the song comes round
    Against the best I can hold my ground,
I'm like the 'maté,' that's not much use
  Until its mouth you open.

Since the choice of the riddle is up to you,
  As stiff as you like please choose it;
    I'm not looking worried, you must allow,
    And I'll answer you now as I best know how:
Law was made as a switch for the poor and rich
  But only the poor man rues it.

The spider's web, it seems to me,
　The law pretty fairly matches.
　　It doesn't bother the rich one bit,
　　Nor the bosses whose job is applying it;
The big beetle breaks it and gets away,
　It's the little bug it catches.

The rain doesn't fall just the same on all,
　And no one can be the chooser;
　　The man that's soaked will sore complain,
　　But the fact of the matter's surely plain;
Which is this: that the Law is like the knife,
　It doesn't hurt the user.

You'll hear some say that the Law's a sword,
　Which isn't a thing for wonder—
　　The man that's got the hilt in hand
　　Sees well where the cut is going to land,
It falls on the fellow that's underneath,
　Unless he gets out from under.

The parts of the doctors of the Law,
　I don't doubt or hold in scorn;
　　I'm a plain-spoken darkie, as you see,
　　And every day clearer it seems to me,
The only law that they're giving us
　Is the little end of the horn.

Martin Fierro.
I'm telling you, darkie, once again,
　I've taken your style and measure,
　　Some good horse-sense out of life you've squeezed;
　　To have run up against you I'm mighty pleased;
To hark to your stuff is more than enough
　To make this match a pleasure.

It's my duty too, to say to you,
  That your brag you've justified.
    I'll tell the truth and shame the devil;
    There's not many singers touch your level,
And though you're pitch dark on the outer bark,
  You're chock-full of light inside.

And I won't have it said I was so ill-bred
  As to here abuse your patience,
    You've answered me, and if now you want
    To know anything that you're ignorant;
Just feel yourself free to puzzle me
  Without any reservations.

        The Nigger.
Good tongue; don't trip or halt or slip,
  Your cunning don't start forgetting;
    Though the stake of the game is a singer's fame,
    It's by missing the mark one learns to aim;
If you go to sea by your own sweet will,
  It's silly to fear a wetting.

I'll ask you now what I'd like to know
 Since to answer me is your pleasure;
  I'll give you best in our singing-match,
  If you answer this batch with all despatch:
Explain to me please what Number is,
 And Time, and Weight, and Measure.

The stake you'll win if you now begin
 Without any hesitation;
  I must tell you clear that what these things are,—
  Though maybe you'll think it's singular—
There's nobody ever has given me yet,
 A downright explanation.

To tell me this all the books I've got
 Are so much useless lumber,
  Your wisdom now may enlighten me
  And your answer my future guide shall be.
So first of the lot, tell me on the spot:
 Why God created Number.

Martin Fierro.

This nigger has got the 'carancho' beat—
 The way he swoops on his nest—
  I can see for this meeting you've come prepared;
  But my wit's not dusty, and I'm not scared.
Let's see if pat I can answer that
 Get ready to give me best.

The sun is one, and the world is one,
 One moon in the sky we see;
So it's plain and broad, that Almighty God
 Never made any quantity.

The One of all ones is a single whole,
   And One was the first amount;
Number only began to be made by man
   As soon as he learned to count.

The Nigger.

Here goes another to test your wits,—
   On this riddle employ your leisure:
      The being that first made One from Nought
      No doubt on his files the answer's got;
But as for me, I never did see
   Just why He created Measure.

Martin Fierro.

Hark well to me—if you don't agree,
   Let my ignorance be excuse—
Every single measure man measures with,
   Man made for his private use.
It's easy to see God didn't need
   Any measure to help his plan,
He had nothing to measure, once he'd fixed
   The length of the life of Man.

The Nigger.

If you answer me this one I'll confess
   In this art you fair excel me;
      A singer of parts has got to know
      Lots of things like these, if he'd make a show;
There's another thing here I want made clear:
   The meaning of Weight please tell me.

Martin Fierro.

God keeps in the store of His secret lore
   This mystery profound;
He simply ordained that every weight
   Should fall till it hit the ground.

And since life is a bundle of bad and good,
  I'll answer you this again:
The use of weight is to estimate
  The sins of the sons of men.

The Nigger.
You'll win if you answer this other one
  With proper rhymes and reasons;
    I'll give you my hand for the best I've met,
    And answer me quick or you lose the bet:
When was Time first made, and why it's split
  Into night and days and seasons?

Martin Fierro.
I'll tell you, darkie: It seems to me,—
  Though your question is troublesome—
That Time is only the tarrying
  For what is about to come.
There was never a time before Time was,
  And it's always got to be,
For Time goes round like a turning wheel
  And a wheel's like Eternity.
If man splits time into then and now,
  This reason I only give:
It's to know how long he's already lived,
  And how long he has yet to live.

I've answered you, but he doesn't win
  Who draws blood in the opening bout;
    If you've got a question up your sleeve,
    Or forgotten something, you've got my leave,
I'm always at hand at your command,
  To decide your slightest doubt.

I'm not saying this to air my brains,
  Though of sense I'm not short of smatters;
    A first-rate singer has got to show
    He's got lots of wind in reserve; and so
  I'll put you through your facings now
    In certain Estancia matters.

Hold on now, nigger, and clear your wits,
  Get set for a nasty jar;
    Don't let your tongue at this question fail,
    And give me your answer on the nail:
  What's got to be done on a cattle-run
    In the months that are spelt with 'r'?

The Nigger.
Of the ignorance of any man
  No man ought to make a mock,
    I'm ready enough to own I'm beat,
    When a singer that's got more class, I meet,
  But I'll make it clear, I didn't come here,
    To be used as a chopping-block.

I've said that in learning got from books
  I don't know 'O' from 'J,'
    You're aiming to make me look a fool,
    And it's not my way to stand ridicule;
  It gets my gall, if with me for ball
    Any man should try to play.

It's only right that in every race
  The quicker should lift the prize;
    It's bound to happen to every one,
    A losing race some day to run,
  When a middling singer makes a match,
    With another of outside size.

Have you ever seen on the open plain
  A man that has lost his way?
    In a daze he wanders to and fro,
    But where to make for he doesn't know;
If you have, you'll know how a singer feels
  When he feels he's going stale.

The trees of the forest creak and groan
  When they're struck by the stormy blast;
    Is it any wonder that here I grieve
    And a heavy sigh from my breast I heave,
When my singer's renown to the wind is blown,
  And my day is overcast?

I swear to heaven from this day on
  I'll give up the singing art;
    And if some day my breast takes fire
    With the olden flame and the old desire,
It won't be my aim to sing for fame,
  But to lighten my heavy heart.

When hope goes west life's lost its zest
  And the world grows wearisome;
    Take this advice: don't hold too fast,
    To anything that's not made to last;
If a poor man gets some happiness
  It's a warning of pains to come.

As long as I live I'll not forget
  The taste of this bitter cup;
    Though time may soften my sorrowings
    Yet never again I'll spread my wings;
If you're not meant to fly in the great blue sky,
  What good is it looking up?

And I'll ask you all that hark to me
  To bear with me still a spell;
    When to come to this party I felt inclined
    It wasn't just singing I had in mind,
But also because beside of that,
  I'd a duty to do as well.

I've told you here that my mother dear,
  Ten sons she bore and bred,—
    But the eldest and best beloved of all,
    Met an evil death; in a tavern brawl
That he didn't start, many years agone,
  By a ruffian's knife he bled.

The nine of us that are yet alive,
  Like orphans he left behind;
    Since then all unconsoled we grieve
    For our brother's loss, you may well believe;
And the man at whose hand he met his death,
  We've not had the luck to find.

Let the bones of my brother rest in peace,
  In the grave they lie quiet and still;
    To stir them up I don't aim to-day,
    But if things should begin to move that way,
I hope God helps me to pay in full
  This long outstanding bill.

If you'd finish this match some other time,
  I'm waiting for your commands;
    And with all the respect that is your due,
    I want right now to suggest to you
That we'll sing if you please of the wrongful deaths,
  Some men have on their hands.

And I'll say to all you gentlemen,
　　As I'm on the point of leaving,
　　　　That the dead man's brothers still survive,
　　　　And all of them very much alive.
And a memory isn't quick to die
　　When it's kept alive by grieving.

What's going to be is a mystery
　　That Time in its bosom guards;
　　　　To say what the next act's going to be,
　　　　Ask a fortune-teller,—don't ask me,—
The future hides what Fate decides,
　　But we'll all know afterwards.

　　　　　Martin Fierro.
Thank goodness at last you've shut your beak,
　　I'll say you can fairly spout;
　　　　I began to suspect a good time back,
　　　　When I saw all those fancy airs you pack,
You'd got something stuck inside your crop
　　And were longing to spit it out.

And now that we know just how we stand
　　For more talk I'm not inclined;
　　　　The chance you're wanting to come your way
　　　　You can have if you like this very day,
It seems to me it's time to begin
　　A match of a different kind.

No more than you can I tell you true
　　What's now about to be;
　　　　But I'm not getting off the trail I choose;
　　　　Till I get to the end, I'll win or lose.
There's never a man since the world began
　　That escapes his destiny.

It was first the grudge of an unjust judge,
    Then the wars of the far frontiers;
        And when I was free of the frontier hell,
        The filthy camps of the infidel;
And now it's this pack of darkies here
    To amuse my declining years.

Their mother put ten of them in the world,
    Which nobody does with ease;
        A woman like that isn't through, I'll bet,
        Perhaps we'll see the poke-shakings yet;
The 'mulita's' litter is always odd,
    And they're all as alike as peas.

With men of colour I never yet
    Found it good to be too polite;
        When their monkey's up their temper's vile,
        They're always ready to spill their bile,
They put me in mind of the spider kind
    All ready and set to bite.

A bunch of quarrelsome nigger boys
    In my times I guess I've met.
        There were some top-notchers among them too,
        Quick of eye and hand, I'm telling you—
If I'm spared—Aijuna! they'll get from me
    ₒA . . . story they won't forget.

But every man has got to pull
    In the yoke he's harnessed to;
        It's a long time now since I picked a fight,
        And in quarrelling I don't delight,
But I'm not afraid of a threatening shade
    Or a wandering bug-a-boo.

I thought that only the bones were left,
　　But I've still got to do the tail;
　　　　By what I can see, it seems to me
　　　　From this racket I simply can't shake free,
　　And I'll tell you all, this is what I call
　　　　To rivet a well-driven nail.

XXXI

MARTIN FIERRO AND HIS SONS GO OFF TO
CAMP ON THE PLAINS

WHEN of bandying words they had made an end,
There was trouble brewing as clear as light;
But some of the company came between,
And before it started they stopped the fight.
When things again were all serene,
Martin Fierro called the boys aside;
They loosed their mounts from the hitching rail
And step by step with a proper pride,
For the open plains they took the trail.

Together they rode till the crimson west,
Shot its dying ray o'er the prairie's breast,
And there by a stream their steeds they reined;
Unsaddled; and then as the daylight waned,
On the ground they sat in a friendly ring,
And talked long hours of many a thing;
For absence has many a tale to tell,
How this came about, and how that befell.
Then they laid them down, and they passed the night,
While high overhead the stars shone bright
In the sky, that's a roof that's denied to none
Of the wanderers underneath the sun.
And of all men never another one
Like the gaucho knows how to make his bed
On the open plain with the sky o'erhead.
When some grassy spot by the trail he's found,
He spreads his saddle-gear on the ground,
The leather 'carona' first; then next,
oThe 'lomillo' for his pillow's fixed,
And the woolly pelt of the saddle-seat,
Covers all, like a mattress soft and sweet,—
Then wrapped in his 'poncho' against the dew,
He sleeps safe and sound the whole night through.
His keen 'facón' by his side he lays,—
For it's never unwise to keep wary ways,—
Bit and quirt at hand, while his horse crops round,
With the lasso-ring buried in the ground.
(Though it's not to your credit altogether,
oAs a rule with the lasso your horse to tether.)
Like that, the night he will dream away,
Till the first faint tint of the dawning day;
And if far off in the wilds he lies
He knows how to guard against surprise,

And safer than under his own roof-tree,
He snores as he likes, loose-legged and free;
There's no bugs there; you can roll around,
You can't fall off from the solid ground,
The earth is a bed that's good and wide,
And no one that wants to come in's denied.
And furthermore you can pass the night
As pleases you best till the morning's light,
And night after night without a care
You sleep out there in the great wide air.
And then in the pink of the peeping day,
All the birds on their pipes begin to play,

For his dreams aren't apt to be over-deep,
Who supperless lays him down to sleep.
A merry time that night they passed
Who after long years had met at last,—
When the heart is happy you'll find it true,
The whole world seems to be happy too.
But their luck was out, they were all poor men,
And each had to fend for himself again;
So they found it best their band to break
And each his separate trail to take,
Till they found some door that would take them in
And work to do that their bread might win.
But before they scattered here and there
To start new lives some other where,
In the morning-hush of the great green plain
Martin Fierro spoke to his boys again,
And to Cruz's son, ere they said farewell,
These words of advice that here I tell.

XXXII

COUNSELS OF MARTIN FIERRO TO HIS SONS

WHEN a father gives counsels to his sons,
   He's a friend and a father too;
     As a friend, my boys, then hark to me:
     In every thing you must wary be,
You're never aware just when and where
   Some enemy waits for you.

The only schooling I ever had,
   Was a life of suffering;
     Don't be surprised if at the game,
     I've made mistakes;—that's not my shame—
It's mighty little a man can know,
   If he's never learnt anything.

There's heads with books stuffed chock-a-block,
   Every breed and brand and style,
     Though I'm not expert in such mysteries,
     I've picked up enough to teach me this:
That better than learning no-end of things
   Is to know a few things worth while.

There's nothing you do will profit you
   If no teaching it has dispensed you;
     A man at a single glance should know
     Just how things stand, and why they're so;
And it's worth a mint not to need a hint
   When you're setting folks against you.

Don't pin all your hopes on any heart
　　Although you may think it's true;
　　　　When under the feet of Fate you're trod,
　　　　Hold firm your faith in Almighty God,
Of men set your trust in only one,
　　Or at very most in two.

The defects of men are common ground,.
　　They've got no boundaries;
　　　　In the very best some fault you'll find,
　　　　So this advice take well to mind:
There's none so good that for other folks
　　Shouldn't make some allowances.

If your friend's in need, be his friend in deed,
　　Never leave him in the lurch;
　　　　But don't ask him for what you lack,
　　　　Or load your troubles on his back.
The truest friend that a man can have
　　Is a name that's got no smirch.

Don't fear to lose; don't scheme to gain,—
　　That won't get you anywhere;—
　　　　However much you may thraw and threep,
　　　　The goods you get you can't always keep.
Don't go with a gift to a rich man's door,
　　Or refuse with the poor to share.

Even infidels will treat you well
　　If you give every man his due;
　　　　Don't be too ready to get annoyed,
　　　　And extra trouble you'll thus avoid;
Don't put on airs among timid men;
　　With the brave let your words be few.

To work is the law, since the human kind
Must be clothed and housed and fed;
Don't let yourselves fall on evil days,
By lazing around in slip-shod ways,
The heart is sore that from door to door
Has to beg for its daily bread.

By the toil of his hands man gets his bread,
And salts it well with weeping,
For poverty doesn't lose a chance
To take advantage of circumstance;
Want lies in wait outside every gate
And slips in if it finds you sleeping.

Don't threaten a man, for there's never one
Won't turn if too hard you goad;
Don't talk big words, to intimidate,—
Or maybe you won't have long to wait
To find you've one quarrel on your hands,
And another one on the road.

To front a danger or come off clear
From the traps of evil chance,—
I tell you this from experience:
Your best stand-by is self-confidence;
To trust yourself is a surer arm
Than any sword or lance.

A moderate bit of mother-wit
All men that are born possess,
Though without it no man could get very far,
I've noted this queer particular:
That the same mother-wit that makes one man wise,
Turns in others to craftiness.

When a chance comes by, the man that's spry
   Takes hold of it on the spot:
      Remember well what I'm telling you,
      You'll find this picture of Chance is true,—
Like the iron that's on the anvil laid,
   It's got to be hit while hot.

There are many things that are lost and found
   In the daily affairs of men,
      But one of the lessons I've learned is this,—
      And fix it well in your memories,—
If you lose your shame, it's lost for good,
   For you won't get it back again.

To stick to your brother's a good old law
   That'll help you in many dangers;
      Remember it boys, and hold together
      In fair as well as in stormy weather,
When a family fight among themselves
   They're soon eaten up by strangers.

Respect grey hairs, for to mock at age
   Is no matter for admiration;
      Whene'er among stranger folk you be,
      Take care how you choose your company,
For a man that picks up with a scurvy crowd
   Gets an evil reputation.

When the stork grows old its sight gets dim
   Till at last its eyes go blind;
      Its little ones keep it in the nest,
      And to care for its age they do their best.
Consider the storks, and learn from them
   This lesson for human kind.

If a man offends,—though you treat it light,
   And the quarrel you don't pursue,
      Be on your guard and keep well alert,
      For whatever happens one thing's a cert:
The man that's done you an evil turn
   Will always talk bad of you.

The man that lives at another's beck,
   Can't expect to live in clover;
      If he does his job with a haughty air,
      He'll get worse treatment and harder fare,
The brisker the hand that's underneath,
   The lighter the hand that's over.

To lose his time, or to lose his shame
   Are the marks of a worthless man,
      Your wits about you always keep,
      And look round well before you leap,
And remember this: there was never a vice
   That ended where it began.

Of all the birds that live by prey,
   The hook-beaked bird is chief;
      But the man that would keep a straight backbone
      Never takes a copper that's not his own,
You may be poor—that's no shame for sure—
   But it's shameful to be a thief.

Keep your hand if you can, from the blood of man,
   Never fight for sheer devilment,
      Let my misery a mirror be,
      And measure yourselves by what there you see;
To know how to hold yourself in hand
   Is a thing that's most excellent.

You'll carry the guilt of the blood you've spilt
   In your heart till death has stilled it,
      The sight of that blood will haunt you so—
      To my grief alas this truth I know—
That it falls like drops of burning fire
   On the soul of him that spilled it.

Wherever you go, you'll not find a foe
   Worse than drink, to stir up trouble;
      I'm telling you this, boys, for your good,
      And I hope you'll remember it as you should:
For a crime that's done by a drunken man,
   The punishment should be double.

In a general brawl and a 'free-for-all,'
   Get out first—it's the only sense;
      Don't carry yourselves with too high an air,
      Although you've got right on your side to spare,
And the man is wise that his knowledge buys
   By other's experience.

If ever a woman you give your heart
   This counsel I recommend:
      Don't do her a turn that will leave her sore,
      Or she'll serve you some day far worse, and more;
For a woman that's wronged won't soon forget,
   And she'll ruin you in the end.

If you want to be singers, feel it first,—
   And you won't have to watch your style;
      Don't ever tune up your strings, my boys,
      Just to hear yourselves, and to make a noise,
But get in the habit, that when you sing,
   It's always of things worth while.

These counsels true I give to you,
　　To learn them has cost me dear;
　　　I've pointed you out the way to go
　　　So you'll never say that you didn't know,
But to give you the grit to follow it
　　Is not up to me—that's clear.

Of the lessons I've learnt in my lonely days
　　These things that I've told are some;
　　　In all this advice that I've given to you,
　　　There's nothing that tested you won't find true;
It's out of the mouth of the hoary-head
　　That the wisest counsels come.

XXXIII

THE LEAVE-TAKING

THEN the four of them to the four wide winds
    Of heaven resolved to scatter;
      A promise among them there they passed,
      To carry it out each bound him fast,
But I can't tell what the promise was,
    For they kept it a secret matter.

The only thing clear I can tell you here—
    And don't let it cause you wonder—
      For many a time a man must act
      As they did then—I just note the fact—
That each of them took a different name
    From the one men had known him under.

I haven't a doubt they did it without
    The slightest of wrong intention;
      Though the naked truth is, all the same,
      When a man picks out a brand-new name,
That the old one's got some kind of blot
    That he doesn't want folks to mention.

And now I'll lay down this instrument
    With which I've amused you friends;
      You'll all agree that I've sung a lot,
      And done my best with a tangled knot,
○Like a button of quill that you can't undo,
    Because you can't find the ends.

I've sung my song as I promised you,
    But I'm still feeling rare and rhymy;
      Or to say it in words that a cattle hand,
      Won't need explaining to understand,
I've still got a bunch of rope to slack
    If any one wants to try me.

With these parting words I'll take my leave,
    Without telling you until when;
      The man who's just out for an easy lot
      Will choose his cut at a tender spot;
But I've always cut through the toughest part
    And I'll cut through the tough again.

To the eagle its nest; to the speckled cat
    In wood and brake its bed;
      The fox in some burrow makes its lair,
      But the gaucho wanders here and there
Borne on by the winds of change and chance,
    With no place to lay his head.

The wretched gaucho's a waif and stray,
    Cast out in the wilds to roam;
      His wrongs never stir a single heart,
      To take up the outcast gaucho's part,
And give him his rights as a citizen,—
    A church, and schools, and a home.

And some day all this tangled tale
  Will come to the end of the telling;
    I'm taking no hand in it anyhow,
    For the carcase is almost pecked by now,
oThe 'chimangos' are busy with beak and claw,
  All perched on the hide and yelling.

But God no doubt will bring some good out
  Of all this stour and seethe,
    And we'll trust in Him that He'll bear in mind
    When He's doing His work with our human kind,
The simple law, that a fire, to draw,
  Must be lighted from underneath.

The man at the top's inside his code
  All the best for himself to snap,
    The very men that put him there
    Of taking his favours should beware,
Remember there's blight in the shade that's cast
oBy the tree with a milky sap.

The man that's poor must go slow and sure
  Or they bring him down with a jerk,
    I put like this what I've felt and seen:
    The gaucho's hide is the tough and lean,
That gives the thong for the lasso strong
  That does all the hardest work.

Every word of the tongue that here has sung
  As truth you may all accept;
    What I've told in my song is clear and plain,
    Of greed or of envy I bear no strain,
And the thatch of the 'rancho' will never leak
  Where this book of mine is kept.

I've given of my best; from my well-earned rest
    No longer I'll be enticed;
        To wind up now I won't be long;
        If you count up the cantos of my song,
The last as you see, is thirty-three—
    The very same age of Christ.

And store these words in your memories
    Before to the trail I take me:
        With the task I've started I'm going through
        Until I finish it well and true,
Unless my wit some day should quit,
    Or my life itself forsake me.

And if life fails me, this I know,
    When the news of my death is spread,
        The roaming gaucho, far away
        In the desert lands, will be sad that day,
And a sudden ache in his heart will wake,
    When he knows that I am dead.

For I've told in these songs of my brothers' wrongs,
    Their pains and their misery;
        When the tale of my life is a tale of old,
        My story with pride in their hearts they'll hold,
And I'll live again for my countrymen,
    When they remember me.

Now memory is a quality
    Of a meritorious kind;
        And any now that perhaps suspect
        That I've been aiming at them direct,
Let them know that a man can forget a wrong,
    Though he holds it well in mind.

Yet don't let anyone take offence,
  I don't plan any folks to gall;
    If I've chosen this fashion to have my say,
    It's because I thought it the fittest way,
AND IT'S NOT TO MAKE TROUBLE FOR ANY MAN,
  BUT JUST FOR THE GOOD OF ALL.

NOTES ON THE POEM
MARTIN FIERRO
BY THE TRANSLATOR

NOTES ON THE POEM

The numbers before the Notes refer to the pages of the text. The lines are indicated by the symbol o in the text itself.

PAge 4. *gaucho.* An Argentine plainsman descended from the original Spanish settlers, and gaining his subsistence by raising or herding cattle and horses (see Introduction). The word is of obscure origin, and has been variously derived from *gauderio* (Latin *gaudere,* to enjoy); from the Araucanian *cachú,* comrade; and from *guacho,* Spanish for orphan. The gaucho's social position as illustrated in the poem makes the last derivation the most appropriate, if not the most philologically plausible. The word is commonly used in the Argentine in an extended sense, for an expert in any particular pursuit requiring skill and nerve, etc.

6. *La Pucha!* A euphemism for *la puta* (the whore!), used currently as an exclamation of surprise, wonder, admiration, etc.

7. *maté.* The gourd out of which *yerba,* or the so-called Paraguayan tea, is sucked by means of a metal tube perforated at one end, called the *bombilla.* The maté is filled three-quarters full of yerba and then filled up with boiling water from the kettle. One maté and bombilla is usually shared by a group of friends and any visitor who may drop in, and is passed in turn around the circle.

7. *china.* The gaucho's wife or female companion.

7. *poncho.* The gaucho's cloak; a square piece of cloth, usually of wool, with a slit in the centre for the head. It falls to below the knee, and is at once a garment, a blanket, and a shield in the duel. As the last, it is wrapped around the left arm, and the expert knife-fighter is skilful in unrolling it on the ground as a trap for the unwary foot of his opponent, or in blinding him momentarily with it to give an opening for an attack.

9. *Pampa.* In the Quichúa tongue *pampas* means space. The name was applied by them to the open plains as distinguished from the *Chaco,* or hunting-ground, and it was adopted by the first settlers.

12. *barbecue.* This is called in the Argentine *asado al asador.* A large fire is made, and after the first blaze and smoke have dissipated, the carcase of the animal, usually a sheep, is spread-eagled on an iron spit (*asador*), which is stuck in the ground and bent over the glowing embers. A tin or other receptacle is placed to catch the grease. When the *asado* is ready, each of the company cuts off a portion with his knife. The knife is also the only utensil used in eating the meat, the method being to hold the strip of meat or joint in the left hand, seize a mouth-

ful between the teeth, and sever the meat just outside the lips with a dexterous upward cut. This requires some practice, and a *gringo* may cut his nose if not careful. The other favourite and more peculiarly gaucho method of roasting meat is the *asado con cuero* (roast with the hide on). This is customarily reserved for festivities and ceremonious occasions. The animal should be, correctly, a heifer; and the meat is divided into suitable portions and roasted before a slow fire, with the hide left on, the side with the hide being turned first to the fire, and care being taken not to burn the hair. It requires an expert to prepare it in the proper manner.

12. *caña*. A drink distilled from fruits of various kinds, and originally from the sugar-cane; with a high alcoholic content.

13. *stocks*. Placing in the stocks was a common form of punishment in the country towns and villages of the Argentine up to the later decades of the nineteenth century. Stocks were to be seen in the yard of every country *comisaria*, and the *comisario* had summary powers to inflict this and other punishments, such as staking-out (See Note on page 20).

16. *gringo*. A word of doubtful etymology, applied to foreigners in Latin America generally, with a slight preference towards different nationalities, varying with the locality. In the Argentine it is applied most appropriately to Englishmen or Italians. The word has variously been derived from 'greenhorn,' from a corrupt version of the opening words of the song, 'Green grow the rushes O,' and from other sources, but it is most probably derived from *griego* (Spanish for Greek), which was used in Spain to indicate a foreigner long before the discovery of America. Though not actually offensive, it contains an element of depreciation.

16. *An English digger of ditches*. Ditches were constructed in many regions of the country, to drain low-lying tracts, and later for irrigation. In 1874 the Government launched a project for the construction of a ditch or fosse over a hundred leagues long, as part of a defence system against the incursions of the Indians; but the scheme was later abandoned owing to its proved inefficacy. The majority of the labourers employed in ditch construction were foreigners. In this passage I have translated as 'an English digger of ditches' the 'ingéls sangiador' of the original, following the explanation given by Eleuterio F. Tiscornia in his ' "Martin Fierro," comentado y anotado.' The word 'sangiador' (correctly 'zangiador' from 'zanja' ditch) does not, however, figure in the Dictionary of the Spanish Academy; and the word for a maker or digger of ditches, should be, if formed analogi-

cally, 'zangero.' The word 'sangiador' is, in the context, susceptible of another interpretation, which is at once more colourful, expressive of one of the well-known peculiarities of the roving Englishman of the period, and illustrates the happy knack of the 'gaucho' in hitting off an idiosyncrasy in a single epithet. 'Sangiador' is still used occasionally by 'paisanos' of the older generation to describe a lean, long-legged person who stalks along, swaying from side to side, and lifting the feet sharply, as if clearing imaginary ditches. The first two lines of the stanza referred to, might in accordance with this interpretation, be translated:

> 'And a long-legged, spring-hocked Englishman
> That had dodged the draft before,' &c.

16. *Inca-la-perra*. A distortion of *Inglaterra* (England). It was a common practice among the country people to substitute an unfamiliar word by one or more words having an approximately equivalent sound. The three words here used, translated literally, mean Inca-the-bitch.

18. *moro*. A dark-coloured horse, almost black. The gaucho appraises a horse largely by its colour, as an indication of its qualities, dark colours being preferred. A white horse is dubbed only fit for harlots. To ride a mare is the last grade of poverty.

18. *Ayacucho*. A small country town in the Province of Buenos Aires, founded in 1867. Like all country towns, it was the scene of periodic race-meetings.

18. *shack*. The gaucho's hut, called in Spanish a *rancho*. The latter word must not be confused with the English word 'ranch,' meaning an *estancia*. The *rancho* is of the most primitive construction, with mud walls and floor, straw roof canted in the centre, windowless and with sometimes only a hide to serve as a door.

19. *bolas*. The most original and characteristic of the gaucho's accoutrements, and one which he adopted from the Indians. It consists of three heavy balls (either of stone or metal) covered with hide and attached to ropes of plaited hide, the ends of which are joined together. It was used in hunting (especially ostriches) and also as a weapon. Thrown at the legs of a running animal, the cords wrap themselves round the legs by the momentum of the balls and effectively truss it up.

19. *lasso*. The gaucho lasso is similar to that in use in other cattle-raising countries.

20. *Barajo!* This is a euphemism for *Carajo!* which is an obscene expletive, much used in the Argentine.

20. *staking-yard.* The stakes, together with the stocks, formed the staple punishments applied by the country *comisarios*, and was carried out in the backyard of the police station. Thongs were tied to the ankles and wrists of the victim and attached to four stout stakes driven into the ground. The thongs were tightened in as far as they would go, and the victim was left, usually for the night.

20. *corral.* An enclosure for horses, close to the buildings of the *estancia*, and usually constructed of rough posts placed upright in the ground.

20. *adobe.* Clay blocks, made in a plank mould, dried in the sun and used in the construction of walls, shacks, etc.

20. *real.* A nickel coin of the value of ten cents. The term is not now current in the Argentine, although in Uruguay, a ten-cent piece is still called a 'real.'

23. *lance.* The Indian lance was usually a stout *tacuara* cane, which is the South American bamboo, and was about six *varas* (eighteen feet) in length, tipped with a blade about a foot long, and adorned about three feet from the blade, with a tuft of ostrich feathers.

25. *gong.* The original word is *cencerro*, which was a primitive bell in the shape of a tube, with a clapper of hardwood or stone, similar to the cattle-bells still to be seen in some parts.

25. *maize.* The aptness of the simile, 'like maize in the toasting-pan,' will be apparent to anyone who has observed the way the grains of maize jump when burst open by intense heat.

26. *Metau el lanza hasta el pluma.* This is 'pidgin-Spanish' for 'I'll stick the lance through you, up to the feathers!' As stated above (Note on page 23), the feathers were attached some three feet beyond the blade.

27. *a lance like a lasso.* The meaning is that the lance was so long that it looked like a lasso.

27. *like the throat of a toad.* Those who have watched a frog or a toad from close at hand while croaking, will appreciate the appropriateness of the figure.

27. *Three Marias.* A pet name used by the gaucho for the bolas. In popular speech the name is also applied to the three stars which form the belt of Orion, one of the most prominent constellations in the sky of the Pampas. In this latter sense it is also employed several times in the poem. (See Note on page 64).

27. *cacique.* The chief of an Indian tribe.

27. *facón.* The gaucho's knife; used as a weapon and also for cutting meat, slaughtering animals, etc. It was originally a cross between a sword and a dagger, possessing the advantages of both, with a straight blade about eighteen inches long, with point and double edge, with a haft of wood, metal or bone, a weapon difficult to improve on for disembowelling an opponent—the gaucho's favourite stroke. To ensure a good grip, it was usual to fit the haft with a covering made of the vein of an animal—hence the pet name of *envenao* often used for the facón. The sheath was often highly ornamented with chased silver. It was carried in its sheath, diagonally across the waist, thrust between the belt and the sash, with the handle to the right. The gaucho never took kindly to fire-arms, and to employ a revolver was considered unvirile. (See Note on page 79.)

28. *boundary-mark.* On the plains these were usually a stone, a heap of earth, etc. Hence the simile.

30. *taba.* A game played with the knuckle-bones of a sheep, similar to the old English game of cockall. It gave rise to so much bloodshed at country gatherings that it was eventually prohibited.

30. *eat grain.* The prairie horse does not eat grain naturally, and has to be taught.

31. *yerba.* Paraguayan tea (see Note on p. 7), the national beverage of the Argentine. It is pleasant to the taste, slightly laxative, is a mental and physical invigorator, and enables the body to undergo long stretches of hunger and fatigue without ill-ease or apparent after-effects.

32. *four.* This number is commonly employed as a synonym for a few, not necessarily four.

32. *Aijuna!* An exclamation signifying amazement, wonder, admiration, etc. It is an abbreviation for the complete phrase, *Ah, hijo de una puta!* for which the literal English would be 'Ah, you whoreson!' used in Shakespeare's day, but now fallen into disuse. *Aijuna!* the Spanish brother to our own phrase, is failing, too, before the encroachments of gentility, and is now chiefly confined in the Argentine to the unlettered, and to a few stalwarts of the older generation. But it has by now become so stereotyped that it has lost much of its offensiveness to delicate ears. It is curious to observe that just the reverse has happened in the case of our English 'bloody.'

32. *as long as a rosary.* In the original Spanish there is a play on words; *cuentas* being not only 'accounts,' but also the beads of a rosary.

34. *Rosas.* Juan Manuel de Rosas was the son of one of the first families of Buenos Aires, born in Buenos Aires in 1793. He managed

his father's estancias in his early manhood, and obtained such ascendancy over the gaucho class that ultimately he drew from them large and semi-disciplined forces with which he became Dictator, and for seventeen years subjected the country to one of the most sanguinary tyrannies in all history. When the tide of rebellion eventually burst the dykes, he fled to England and died as a country gentleman outside Southampton.

35. *guanaco.* The well-known quadruped, sometimes called the sheep of the Andes, domesticated by the Indians and used as a beast of burden and also for its wool. It is very nimble and light on its feet and capable of great speed.

37. *peones.* Spanish for 'labourers'; also applied to estancia 'hands.'

38. *papolitano.* A distortion of *napolitano*, a Neapolitan.

38. *duck of the feast.* A proverbial expression in Spanish, meaning that one has come off with the worst part in any affair.

38. *Quen vívore?* A corruption of the Italian sentry for the challenge, 'Quien vive?'—'Who goes there?'

38. *Qué víboras.* A mocking answer given by Martin Fierro in imitation of the sentry's jargon. The words mean, 'What snakes?'

38. *Ha garto.* The sentry meant to say '*Haga alto!*' a command to halt.

38. *lagarto.* Another mocking repartee. *Lagarto* is a lizard.

43. *Don Gainza.* General Martin de Gainza was Minister for War during the Presidency of Sarmiento, 1868–1874.

43. *scores.* Rifling of cannon, a novelty for the gauchos at the time to which the poem refers. There is a play on words between the 'scores' in this line, and the 'scores' (or accounts) kept by the bar-keeper, in the following verse.

43. *pulpería.* The old type of country store in the villages, colonies and settlements of the Argentine plains. It was at once store, bar, inn, exchange, news-disseminator, general meeting-place and unofficial club. A tether-rail, a covered porch, an earthen floor, a long wooden counter 'marked with many a ding,' backed by a scaffolding of shelves bearing tins and bottles of indefinable commodities, a few casks and cases on the floor, and one or two tables, stools and benches—such was the *pulpería* in its palmy days, the scene of many a dance, many a singing-match between local champions, and many a fight, such as those related in the poem.

43. *on my feet.* When his horse falls by putting its foot in a hole, or throws him while being broken, the gaucho's pride is to come out of the scuffle on his feet, the reins in his hand, and with spurs a-jingle,

ready to turn and swing into the saddle again as the animal struggles up.

45. *lie of the land.* The gaucho was a past-master at finding his way or knowing his whereabouts on the plains under all circumstances. By chewing a little grass every now and then, he could tell whether there was water in this or that direction, and whether it was salt or fresh—also in what part of the country one was, and the bearings to Don So-and-so's estancia. The lie of the grass would, on dark nights, give him his compass points. He could count a company of riders by the sound, and tell you if the horse that left this trail here had a rider, and perhaps who it was likely to be. He could smell houses too by night, far beyond sight or sound of them; and a *tolderia* of Indians by day when it was still below the horizon. This last, however, was the least difficult feat, for the Indian made his tents of green horse-hides and butchered his meat at his own tent-flap, and the odour of the charnel blew to leeward like a banner.

45. *peludo.* This word means 'hairy'; and it is the name applied to a variety of armadillo, chiefly distinguished from the other varieties by having long black hairs. To 'catch a *peludo*' is also slang for getting intoxicated.

49. *press his hat on.* The instinctive gesture of a person in a hurry.

51. *pericón.* A figure dance for four, six, eight or more couples. It is exclusively a national dance of the Argentine, and it appears to have arisen spontaneously among the gauchos, as a mixture of the *gato* (in which the dancers imitate a wild-cat stalking a partridge) and the *güella* (the dance of the throat-cutters of Rosas). Some say that the dance imitates the paces and attitudes, when courting, of the *ñandu*, or South American ostrich. The African negroes who were brought as slaves to the Argentine, called the ostrich chick a *perico*, the termination *on* being an augmentative,—hence the name.

51. *The negroes* were the descendants of African negroes brought to the country as slaves in Spanish colonial times. After their emancipation by the declaration of independence, they enjoyed equal rights with Spanish and 'criollo' Argentine citizens, though remaining socially inferior.

The *Indians* were the aboriginal race dispossessed by the Spanish colonists. They were divided into many tribes and they maintained a ceaseless warfare among themselves and against the invading white man until the 'eighties' of the last century. They were not negroes but of a type approximate to the Indian of North America.

51. *a bit . . . chilly.* The gaucho takes a school-boyish delight in con-

veying veiled meanings or piquant or offensive epithets, by means of liaisons between the words of some ostensibly innocent remark. In the original Spanish, the hidden word is here 'cow' instead of 'bitch,' and the former has more point, in view of a certain physical development of the negress which would make the comparison more appropriate.

52. *ass . . . tute*. This line in the original contains another example of the peculiar form of humour explained above. Nothing could be done with the line literally, and I have inserted the nearest equivalent.

53. *S-shaped*. A guard in the shape of an S was considered the best. (See Note on *facón*, page 27.)

54. *freshly-pupped*. The ferocity of all females, immediately after parturition, is proverbial.

57. *under the eaves*. To ride one's horse right up to the door was looked upon as offensive, or at least as a lack of courtesy.

58. *brother-in-law*. The suggestion conveyed by calling a stranger one's brother-in-law, is evident. Fierro's rejoinder implied, in turn, that the peccant female who had established the relationship, was not his sister, but the other's. It should be mentioned, however, that *cuñao*, 'brother-in-law,' is often used in the Argentine without offence being meant or taken. The swaggering manner and the half-filled flask, nevertheless, make Fierro's attitude consistent.

60. *What good is a bullock*, etc. This is a well-known Spanish proverb. 'Donde ira el buey que no are, sino al matadero?'

61. *wooden bell*. Another proverb, meaning that a poor man's arguments are as little listened to, as the sound of a wooden bell.

63. *vizcacha-lair*. A burrowing animal very common on the plains throughout the Argentine. It constructs warrens of considerable extent, and the excavated earth thus thrown up, forms a slight elevation. The ground over these lairs is naturally softer than the surrounding plain. Large quantities of owls frequent the vizcacha burrows, and have apparently arranged a modus vivendi suitable to both parties.

64. *Three Marias*. In this context the Three Marias are the stars in the belt of Orion—not the 'bolas.'

65. *chajá*. The name of a bird, from the Guarani language, in imitation of its cry. It is a long-shanked bird about the size of a duck, slate-colour crested, with black and white neck. It lives near water; and it is the sentinel and self-appointed guardian of the peace in the vicinity of its habitat, giving the alarm at any intrusion.

66. *sash*. The gaucho swathes his waist with a binder of cloth about six feet long, on top of which is worn the *tirador*, or leather belt, pro-

vided with pockets and sometimes studded with silver coins. The sash forms an excellent support for the bowels and a preventive of rupture, and is also to a certain degree a protection against a knife slash. The cloth itself is, of course, easily cut, but the broad and firmly-swathed binder enables a cure to be obtained in some cases which might otherwise prove fatal.

68. *round their arms.* See under *poncho*, Note on page 7.

68. *tacuara.* The name, adopted from the Guarani language, of a cane. It grows in thick brakes, in the north of the Argentine, and in Paraguay and Bolivia, attaining a height of 25 to 30 feet, and a diameter of six inches. It is the bamboo of South America, and was used by the Indians for making lances.

68. *hitching-rack.* Every *estancia*, *pulpería*, or even humble *rancho*, was provided with its hitching-rack or *palenque*, a horizontal wooden rail raised a few feet from the ground, for tethering horses.

69. *on the ground.* The action of scratching the ground with the knife-point is a customary attitude of the knife-fighter; and is at once a challenge, an invitation to attack, and a feint, equivalent in some degree to the movement of a boxer's hands when facing an opponent and looking for an opening.

69. *killed my lice.* A humorous expression for a slash over the scalp.

71. *stretched their muzzles out.* A slaughtered animal stretches out its muzzle when it dies—hence the popular phrase; equivalent to our expressions: 'kicks its last,' 'stiffen out,' etc.

71. *caranchos.* A species of hawk, a carrion-eater, the scavenger of the plains. Before devouring its find, it walks sedately around it, sweeping the ground with its wings.

74. *how to fall.* To know how to take a fall is the most important part of the horse-breaker's technique. A man may know how to ride, but if he bungles his falls he may break his back or his neck, or go under his horse when it rolls.

76. *rancho.* The gaucho's shack; not to be confused with our word 'ranch,' which is properly applied to an *estancia*, inclusive of its buildings and lands. (See under 'shack,' Note on page 18.)

76. *liver-fluke.* The liver-fluke is frequent in the lagunas and marshlands. This disgusting parasite attacks both beast and man, and anyone who has cut up a liver infested with them will appreciate the aptness of the simile.

77. *half-licked.* When a calf is born the mother licks it all over, especially the head, to free it from the placental mucus. Until she has finished licking it, it presents rather a miserable appearance.

78. *with the flat.* Among knife-fighters, this is a gesture of contempt, implying that the recipient is too harmless to be worth wasting time and trouble on.

79. *fancy gun.* As stated under the reference 'facón,' the gaucho always disdained the use of fire-arms. At the time to which the poem refers, the revolver was a comparative novelty in the Argentine.

79. The references in these lines are to the physical effects of fear.

83. *gato and fandango.* The names of two popular dances.

84. In the original Spanish, the verse comprised by these lines contains a play upon words, which any attempt at translation robs of all point. I have therefore substituted a verse of my own, which has the same tone and a similar intention.

> Hay gauchos que presumen
> De tener damas;
> No digo que presumen,
> Pero se alaban,
> Y a lo mejor los dejan
> Tocando tablas.

88. *a strip off the ribs.* The lean meat between the hide and the ribs is considered a delicacy, called *matambre* or *matahambre*, which means 'hunger-killer.' In the palmy days of the gaucho, when vast herds of semi-wild cattle roamed the Pampas, it was not uncommon for the gaucho to slaughter an animal, take the matambre and the tongue, and abandon the rest of the carcase for the *caranchos.*

89. *criollo.* In Spanish America a *criollo* is the offspring of European parents, born in the country, as distinct from foreign-born immigrants, or half-breeds; not to be confused with the meaning of the word as employed in the United States or in the West Indies.

90. *tero.* A bird similar to the *chajá*, but insectivorous instead of herbivorous. Its name is derived from its call 'teru-teru.' Like our own pee-wit, when disturbed it endeavours to entice the intruder by its call as far as possible from its nest.

93. *as the withered*, etc. When the grass is withered by the sun's heat, the blades turn eastward. In the gaucho poem *Santos Vega* there is a similar passage:

> Siempre caen al marchitarse
> con las puntas al naciente.

93. *matacos, quirquinchos, and mulitas.* Varieties of armadillo.

94. *gaucho ostrich. Gaucho* is here employed as an adjective with the meaning of expert or cunning. (See Note on page 4.)

94. *Three Marias.* Bolas.

100. *Thirty-one.* This is a card game similar to vingt-et-un, much in vogue among the gauchos at the time of the poem. The object of the game is to draw cards totalling exactly thirty-one. Obviously, if a player reaches thirty, he does better to 'stand,' rather than draw, and risk 'bursting.'

101. *weep.* The reference is to the author's avowed intention of re-counting from his actual experience the social injustice of the gaucho's lot, without fear or favour. This motif runs through the entire first canto of *The Return.*

104. *wagon-shaft.* In the old bullock-wagons of the Argentine plains the driver took his seat on the joint of the shaft with the yoke. He was provided with a long cane, with the point of which he could reach the bullocks in front of him, while using the butt on those behind. The use of the goad in this manner serves as an illustration of the power exercised by a local Justice of the Peace. (Cf. page 197, and Note.) As a consequence of the bad condition of the roads and the lumbering and unequal gait of the bullocks, the driver's seat was a precarious one for anyone not made expert by long practice.

108. *Cacique.* An Indian chief.

111. *Huincá.* A Pampa-Indian word meaning 'Christian.'

116. *tilted hands.* In the original *bendito*, literally 'blessed.' A striking metaphor in a single word. Eleuterio F. Tiscornia says in his *Martín Fierro*, Vol. I, page 153: *Bendito* is the opening word of the only prayer the gaucho knows. It was also associated in his mind with the custom of asking a blessing from parents or god-parents. And as in both cases he joined his hands in the gesture of prayer, he had in his mind a ready-made image which Fierro here applies to a tent made out of two mare-hides, suspended from a ridge-pole in the usual shape of all Indian tents. The image would be obscure to English readers unless expanded, as I have done in these lines.

117. *peludo.* In the original *piche*, a variety of 'peludo,' one of the armadillo family.

122. *take in your belt.* In the original *atarse la faja.* The gaucho wore loose drawers, and over these a *chiripá*, a single oblong piece of cloth which passed between the legs and was tucked under his belt before and behind. A needful precaution in preparing for a fight was to tighten the belt (*tirador*) or cloth girdle (*faja*), in order to keep the *chiripá* from working loose and entangling the legs (see page 151, verse 5).

122. *puma.* The South American lion.

123. *laugh.* It seems to be a fact that laughter is a sign of intellectual development. The animal and the primitive savage do not laugh.

123. *animal names.* The Indian braves were baptized with the smoking blood of an animal, and were given names such as *Carimangue,* condor; *Cadupani,* black lion; *Alcluan, guanaco,* etc. (See *Martin Fierro,* by Eleuterio F. Tiscornia, Vol. I, footnote to page 160.)

126. *repartija.* This is a provincial corruption of *reparto* peculiar to the province of Santiago del Estero—hence the allusion to the *Santiagueño,* or native of that province.

127. *skinning-knives.* One of the barbarous customs of the Pampa Indians was the wholesale slaughter of the herds brought back from their forays, for mere lust of blood. In comparison with the number of animals slaughtered, only a few of the hides were used in tent-making and the remainder piled up to rot, thus creating the notorious 'Indian-stench,' which could be felt miles away. When the corruption became too noisome even for the Indian, he moved his camp.

129. *The crow.* These two lines refer to the Biblical story of the raven which was too busy, no doubt, looking for food, to come back to Noah with the tidings of the recession of the flood. (Genesis viii. 7.) In the Scottish language the same image is preserved in the word 'corbie-messenger': a messenger who returns not at all, or too late. (Jamieson's *Dictionary of the Scottish Language.*)

130. *woman's dance.* The description of this 'sport' of the Indian braves seems, by all accounts, to be authentic.

130. *Iokú.* An Indian word, of which I have not been able to trace the meaning.

133. *Gualicho.* The Indian spirit of evil.

144. *Head-flattening.* The Pampa Indians tied their male children in boxes which the mothers carried on their backs when travelling. This had the effect of flattening the back of the head.

149. *misses fire.* The gaucho always had a contempt for fire-arms. (See Note on *facón,* page 27.)

159. *bolas round its feet.* The Pampa Indians trained their horses to such a degree of efficiency that a good horse could often carry its master out of danger even after its fore or hind legs had been trussed together by the deadly 'bolas,' provided the leg-bones had not been broken. Of this several cases are well authenticated.

159. *under the neck.* A favourite trick of the Indian in the fight or the hunt, and one that required a high degree of that co-operation between man and horse which is the kernel of horsemanship.

159. *word-and-hand.* 'Old timers' of the Argentine Pampas (a few of

whom still linger on), who had the opportunity of judging, will tell you that no horse was ever better trained than the Indian mount. These horses were trained by kindness, not by 'savageing.' The 'horse-breaker' was a Christian product for which the infidel had small esteem, not from any innate tenderness towards the animal, but from the standpoint of the adjustment of means to aim,—in this case that of producing a horse capable of responding, with understanding, to every need or predicament of its master.

164. *Ombú*. The most typical tree of the Argentine Pampas. Its botanical name is *Phytolacca dioica*. The trunk is thick and squat, often split up into enormous vertical ridges, the roots extending far around, often at the level of the ground. The limbs are stout, long, and stretch out horizontally, the foliage thick, and of a dark green colour. It is usually found on the open plain, seldom near the gaucho's shack, for a baleful influence was attributed to it in the folklore of the country. (See page 303, and Note.)

183. *maté*. The gourd out of which an infusion of *yerba* is sucked; here used, by extension, for the latter. (See Note on page 7.)

187. *mavericks*. Unbranded calves which are not following a cow. A North American term.

188. *a minor*. In Fierro's time, legal majority was attained at twenty-five. (See Note on page 215.)

189. *chiripá*. A strip of cloth; part of the gaucho's costume; similar to the subligaculum of the Roman gladiator. (See Note on page 122.)

190. *Vizcacha*. A burrowing rodent, native of the Argentine plains. (See Note on page 63.)

190. *moro*. A dark-coloured horse. (See Note on page 18.)

190. *parrots' claws*. A faithful image of the feet of many a wandering gaucho of the old days, among whom it was customary to grip the stirrup between the big toe and the second.

191. *pulpería*. See Note on page 43.

191. *yerba*. See Note on page 31.

191. *the certificate*. The reference is to the certificate of ownership (in this case forged) which was required for the sale of branded hides.

192. *tails of mares*. The particular form of thievery referred to consisted in plucking the hair from the tails of range-mares. The hair commanded a ready market at good prices.

193. *broom-tails*. Range-mares.

196. *drawing brands*. A favourite pastime of the gaucho was that of tracing on the ground with the point of his *facón* or with the finger, the brands of the owners in his district.

196. *lean dogs.* Vizcacha's advice is that where the dogs are starved, their owner is not likely to give the caller a welcome.

197. *devil.* The old saw that Vizcacha repeats is common in Spanish literature:

> El diablo sabe por diablo
> Pero mas sabe por viejo.

197. *the Judge.* The Justice of the Peace in the old days of the Argentine outlands was the virtual ruler of his district, often a bully, bad-tempered and unscrupulous.

197. *spike and butt.* See Note on page 104.

197. *calving-time.* The cow frets when her pasturage is changed and only settles down when she has calved.

198. *runaway.* It is evident that if a runaway animal goes uphill it suffers from two handicaps: it tires itself out, and is more easily visible.

200. *knife-side.* The *facón* was customarily worn stuck through the belt with the haft to the right. Figuratively the advice means that one should not wait for a direct attack, but 'get there first' as soon as an intention to attack is perceived.

200. *drag at the hilt.* Don't take out your knife unless you intend to use it.

200. *pot-belly.* The original has literally, 'If a man is born with a pot-belly, it is useless to cinch him in.' (One cannot escape from one's innate qualities or defects.)

202. *culandrera.* The correct word is *curandera*: a female quack-doctor, a familiar figure in every district in Fierro's time, expert in remedies which were a strange medley of nature-lore, superstition, mother-wit, and pretension.

202. *tabernacle.* The artful 'wise-woman' could not risk her prestige by using every-day speech for her diagnosis. A swelling in the armpit became a 'tubercule under the omoplate,' and 'tubercule' was transformed into 'tabernacle' by the illiteracy of the narrator. Hence the passage-at-arms which follows between him and the learned interrupter.

205. *Alcalde.* Spanish for Mayor.

206. *bury the heads.* The object of burying the heads was to destroy the means of identifying the stolen fleece, sheep being marked with dye on the face or head.

207. *Barullo.* The word means a row, a racket, a rumpus, etc.

212. *scapulary.* It was a custom, common among the gauchos, who

were always religious, to wear a scapulary suspended over their shoulders under their clothing.

213. *peon*. A labourer, or estancia-hand.

215. *masterless man*. The original has *moro sin señor* (an ownerless horse), but Eleuterio F. Tiscornia advances cogent reasons in favour of 'moro' being a misprint for 'mozo.'

215. *thirty years old*. The judge was taking advantage of the youth's ignorance of the law, to assure himself the disposal of his property. (See Note on page 188.)

216. *fortune-teller*. Another typical character of the old times, specimens of which still exist, though now restricted in their activities. 'A wizard full of charms and philtres, a reader of signs and stars, companion of the bat and owl, a black cat his familiar.'

220. *Knave*. To 'see the knave coming out' is an expression taken from a card game, in which to be dealt the knave was bad luck, the holder of the knave at the end of the game being the loser.

223. *Picardía*. A word meaning 'Roguery.'

224. *carancho*. The scavenger-birds of the Pampas. (See Note on page 71.)

224. *Santa Fé.* The town of Santa Fé, capital of the Argentine Province of the same name.

225. *Articulos de la Fé*. The Articles of the Roman Catholic Faith.

226. *Articulos de Santa Fé*. A reference to the coloured girl, a native of Santa Fé, which scarcely requires an extended explanation.

227. *chucho*. Marsh-fever, characterized by shivering and cold sweats.

227. *San Camilo*. One of the saints in the Roman Calendar. *Camilucho*, is a depreciative name used by the gaucho to signify a man of poor spirit, and it evidently came off the young man's tongue when his attention was distracted, as more familiar to him than the name of the saint.

227. *entripation*. A word not in the dictionary, but formed by analogy from a word much more current in the gaucho's vocabulary than the one he was asked to repeat.

229. *Crane*, etc. This is a proverb, meaning simply that it is better to get out of a bad position, even if there are difficulties in the way of doing so.

230. *sanding or stacking a deck*. To sand a deck of cards is to mark them secretly; to stack is to arrange them in a desired manner while appearing to shuffle them. (Sharper's slang.)

230. *flap a jay*. Slang: to cheat a victim at cards.

230. *bunco-game.* Cheating at cards (slang).

230. *rake the pot.* Lift the stakes (slang).

230. *salted pack.* A prepared pack (slang).

230. *pigeon.* A sharper's victim (slang).

230. *broads.* Playing-cards (slang).

230. *bonnet.* A confederate (slang).

231. *gate.* A bottom card, about to be laid on the table in some card-games (slang).

231. *give him rope.* The reference is to roping cattle. When the noose has settled round the head or horns, the coils are paid out till the appropriate moment to give the jerk and bring the animal up.

231. *aces and threes.* The ace and the three are held to be the luckiest cards, and to lose on them is a sign that one is a tyro or that one's luck is at the lowest ebb.

232. *top-shuffle the deck and shift the cut.* This is to make a show of shuffling while leaving the cards in their pre-arranged positions; then to allow the opponent to cut and by sleight-of-hand to nullify his cut.

232. *truco.* A card-game, peculiar to the Argentine and Uruguay, though each has its special modifications of the game. It is a wittier and more difficult game than bridge or whist, and calls for extraordinarily nimble wits, skill in bluffing, and long practice. Persiflage and repartee, often in extemporized verse, form part of the game, and it is an entertainment in itself to watch and listen to experts.

233. *high-men and low-men.* Doctored dice, arranged to turn up high or low (slang).

233. *ringing the changes.* Giving false money for the stakes (slang).

233. *taba.* A gambling game, played with a bone.

235. *Santa Lucia.* One of the saints of the Roman Calendar, supposed to have eyesight under her special care.

235. *ma gañao con picardia.* Gringo-jargon for *me ha gañado con picardia;* 'he has won by trickery.'

236. *ñato.* A nick-name, meaning 'pug-nose.'

237. *Co . . . mo . . . quiando.* A play on words. The first four syllables contain the word *moquiando,* which means 'mocking;' and the whole phrase, when shorn of this double meaning, is equivalent to, 'As I would like to listen to a singer.' . . .

237. *ña . . . to . . . ribia.* Another play on words, enclosing the insult *ñato.* Ña is here an abbreviation for 'Doña,' and the name of the lady who was being addressed was 'Doña Toribia.'

238. *bones.* It was customary to use bones as fuel for the fires.

239. *San Ramon.* Ramon Nonato, a Spanish cardinal (1204-1240),

canonized in 1414. He was brought into the world by hysterotomy, and as a consequence, no doubt, of this circumstance women in child-birth are confided to his special protection. The reference in these lines is to the image of the saint, which was usually stowed away in some obscure corner of the gaucho's dwelling except at the times when his help was invoked.

259. *pack braid.* A reference to the 'brass-hats.'

260. *La Bruja.* 'The Witch.'

261. *ka-me, ka-thee.* 'Scratch my back and I'll scratch yours' (Pro-vincial English).

262. *compañero.* Comrade.

262. *puchero.* The national dish of the Argentine countryman; con-sists of boiled meat and an assortment of vegetables, cooked and served together.

270. *Ten.* The number 10 was supposed to be specially favoured by Providence.

270. *macá.* An aquatic bird, that often can be seen carrying its chicks on its back while swimming.

272. *J from O.* The original has 'I don't know the J, because it's round.' The darkie uses this absurd image to make a show of the illiteracy he is claiming, perhaps in order to use as an alibi if he is worsted. I have substituted a similar image, but one more easily in-telligible to English readers. The original Spanish saying is 'not to know the O, because it is round' *(no conocer la O por redonda)*. Equiva-lent to the English phrase, now obsolete, 'not to know a B from a Battledore,' battledore being an old name for a school hornbook.

288. *mulita's litter.* The *mulita*, a small animal of the armadillo family, is said always to have an odd number at a birth. The insult is particularly deadly, as the *mulita* is notorious for its timidity.

288. *a . . . story.* The implication is a 'lesson,' or a *paliza* (a licking) instead of 'story.'

291. *carona and lomillo.* These are parts of the gaucho's saddle, which is of the 'built-up' variety.

291. *tether with the lasso.* One way of tethering a horse on the open prairie was to fasten him to the lasso and bury the ring at the end of it under the ground. The lasso should not be used thus, however, ex-cept in exceptional cases.

302. *buttons of quill.* Spanish, *boton de pluma,* or literally, 'feather-button.' Among the primitive arts of the Indians of the Pampas was that of manufacturing buttons from the quills of ostrich-feathers. The quill was split lengthwise and the strips were plaited with much in-

genuity to form a button, the ends being tucked in so that they were invisible. (Usually used as fastenings on horse-gear.) Such buttons are now made of leather thongs or sinews; and the *boton de pluma* has become a relic of the past.

303. *chimangos.* A carrion bird; one of the scavengers of the Pampas. It is here cited as an image of the self-seeking politicians and the corrupt officialdom which in the early days of the Republic oppressed and exploited the gaucho class.

303. *tree with a milky sap.* Spanish, *arbol que da leche.* In the folklore of the gaucho, an influence baleful to human beings lurked in the shadow cast by a tree having a milky sap, such as the fig-tree, the eucalyptus, and the *ombú.*